Leading the Way

Leading the Way

Women in Power

Senator Janet Howell and Theresa Howell

foreword by Hillary Rodham Clinton

illustrated by Kylie Akia
and Alexandra Bye

CANDLEWICK PRESS

"You can't dream unless you know what the possibilities are."
— Supreme Court Justice Sonia Sotomayor

I dedicate this book to my mother, Elsie Lightbown Denison, and my mother-in-law,
Ruth Rea Howell. Each broke down barriers to women's success. Elsie offered
job-training opportunities for female federal prisoners. Ruth wrote books for city
children about the science around them. They both overcame societal obstacles and soared.
J. H.

For Ella and Sylvia, and for all the women in our lives and in this book who have
bravely stood up, spoken out, and made a difference. You continue to inspire us.
T. H.

First, I would like to thank all the amazing women, past, present,
and future, who inspire, dream big, and continuously conquer obstacles.
I would also like to thank everyone who supported me in illustrating this book
and those who continue to push me toward my dreams.
K. A.

To Sue, for her integrity, persistence, diligence, empathy,
resourcefulness, courage, communication, and relentless dedication
to students and the community for thirty-two years.
A. B.

Text copyright © 2019 by Janet Howell and Theresa Howell. Foreword copyright © 2019 by Hillary Rodham Clinton. Portrait illustrations copyright © 2019 by Kylie Akia. Other illustrations copyright © 2019 by Alexandra Bye. Illustration of Patsy Mink (p. 66) based on a photograph, used with permission of Gwendolyn Mink. All rights reserved. No part of this book may be reproduced, transmitted, or stored in an information retrieval system in any form or by any means, graphic, electronic, or mechanical, including photocopying, taping, and recording, without prior written permission from the publisher. First edition 2019. Library of Congress Catalog Card Number 2019940095. ISBN 978-1-5362-0846-7. This book was typeset in Chaparral Pro. The illustrations were created digitally. Candlewick Press, 99 Dover Street, Somerville, Massachusetts 02144. visit us at www.candlewick.com
Printed in Stevens Point, WI, USA. 19 20 21 22 23 24 WOR 10 9 8 7 6 5 4 3 2 1

Praise for
Leading the Way

"We learn and become inspired by example, and what better examples for girls than the brave and barrier-breaking women in *Leading the Way*? The women profiled here were once girls who not only dreamed big but went big. These women from different backgrounds, in different circumstances, chose to lead, and I hope the young readers of this book do the same!"

— **Former Secretary of Homeland Security Janet Napolitano**

"Children often grow up aspiring to the jobs they see people like them doing. I am thrilled that *Leading the Way: Women in Power* will show today's children the long legacy of women who have led and continue to lead their communities — and who opened doors for them to do the same. Inspiring more young women to be politically active makes this book important to our future!"

— **U.S. Senator Tim Kaine**

"It is so important that we inspire young people to become active in politics. The fifty women in this book are groundbreaking role models for our kids."

— **U.S. Congresswoman Jennifer Wexton**

Contents

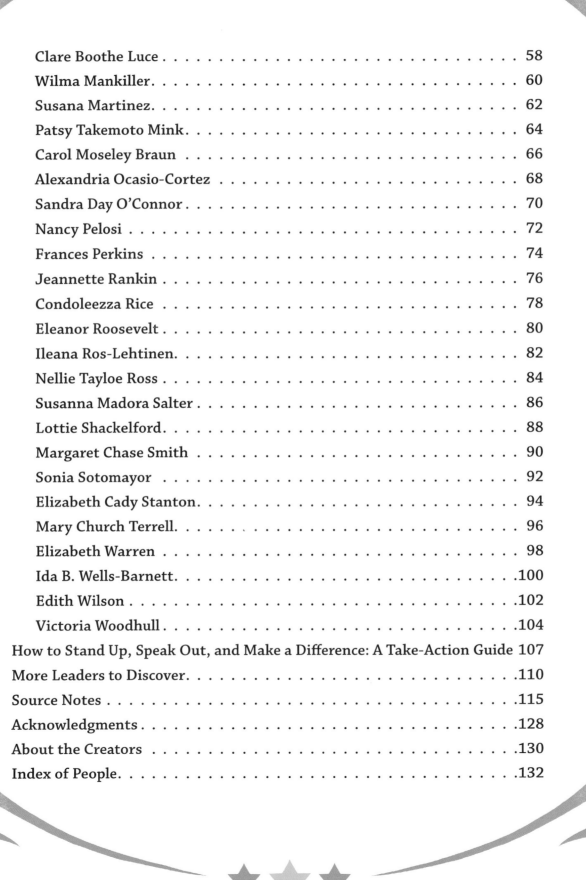

Foreword

by Hillary Rodham Clinton

2020 MARKS ONE HUNDRED YEARS since women won the right to vote in the United States. That may seem like forever if you're a kid, but in the context of history, it wasn't all that long ago that women had no official say in decisions that governed our lives.

My mother, Dorothy, was born before women could vote. But she lived long enough to have the chance to vote for her own daughter in a presidential primary. That remarkable progress took place over the course of one life span, but it didn't just happen. For decades before she was born and throughout her life, courageous women risked their own reputations, even their lives, for the right to participate in their government. These fierce, bold, and persistent women through the generations led the way.

Today, women in America not only have the right to vote but are also able to run for office and participate in all aspects of life precisely because of the hard work, devotion, and sacrifices of those who came before us—women like Elizabeth Cady Stanton and Ida B. Wells-Barnett, who fought for women's suffrage and were some of the first women to run for public office; Soledad Chávez Chacón, the first Latina elected to statewide office; Jeannette Rankin, the first woman elected to Congress; and Shirley Chisholm, who famously said: "If they don't give you a seat at the table, bring a folding chair."

We need not look exclusively to history for inspiring examples of women who have done just that; we can look to our current headlines. In the midterm elections of 2018, a record number of over one hundred women won seats in the United States Congress — each proudly owning her ambition and realizing her desire and conviction to make a difference. Young women activists continue to be on the forefront of standing up to fight for sensible gun violence prevention measures and bold action to meet the challenge of global climate change.

Leading the Way: Women in Power is a tribute to women — past and present — who have blazed trails and shaped history to become some of the bravest and most influential leaders in America — breaking glass ceilings, making a difference, and refusing to be silenced.

Every time a woman stands up and claims what has been a historically male space, she carves a path for others to follow. I was inspired to pursue public service by the example of women in my own life: my mother, my teachers, mentors — from Marian Wright Edelman to Barbara Mikulski — and role models like Eleanor Roosevelt.

I'm humbled to think that I follow in the footsteps of these heroines, among others. I hope that my own career as an advocate, lawyer, First Lady of Arkansas, First Lady of the United States, U.S. senator, U.S. secretary of state, and presidential candidate will serve as a reminder to women and girls today that the sky is the limit when it comes to fulfilling their own potential.

Forging change and, yes, leading the way, is not always easy, but it is *always* worth it. Throughout my life, I have been privileged to meet incredible women and girls from all walks of life and all across the world. I've done my best to encourage and spur them on, and I've also learned from them. Together, we can build a better, stronger, and fairer future; it just takes vision and the tenacity to make that vision a reality.

As you will learn from reading about the women in this book, sometimes it's the little things you do that can make a big difference. Some of these leaders started simply by hanging posters or giving speeches. Others wrote letters and articles. Some organized people together, and some stood up alone.

As you find your own way forward, always remember to dream big, work hard, and be persistent. If you stumble, keep faith, get right back up, dust yourself off, and keep going. And above all else, never stop believing in your dreams and remember that the world is waiting for you to lead the way.

Introduction

IT IS AMAZINGLY POWERFUL to see women in roles of leadership. If girls can see it, they can believe it. They know they can become it.

This book is not about a specific political party or agenda. It's about powerful women who, despite enormous challenges, have bravely stood up, spoken out, and broken new ground. It's a call to action and an important introduction to the political role models, across the political spectrum, who have helped pave the way for the future leaders of America — both boys and girls — especially in a time where there is still ground that needs to be broken.

It's remarkable to think that as of 2020, women will have had the right to vote in the United States for only one hundred years. Before that, women had no voice, no platform, to bring about political change or to weigh in on matters that affected their lives deeply. For decades, courageous women fought to change that because women wanted a voice. They wanted to be heard. They wanted to make a difference.

They wanted to lead.

Before women could vote, before they were allowed to be politicians and judges, women had to find other ways to let their voices be heard. "My pen runs riot," Abigail Adams wrote in the year 1797. Adams wrote hundreds of letters expressing her hopes for her new nation. She argued for a country where girls received the same education as boys and where women could run for political office. Like so many others, Adams had the vision but not the power to make it a reality.

Over one hundred years later, Jeannette Rankin actively fought for votes for women, won that right, ran for political office, and became the first woman ever elected to Congress. Talk about an uphill climb!

From Abigail Adams to Jeannette Rankin to Shirley Chisholm, the first black woman elected to Congress, to Bella Abzug, who declared, "This woman's place is in the House . . . the House of Representatives!" to Sandra Day O'Connor, the first woman to sit on the Supreme Court, women have been taking risks, defying expectations, and making real change in our country. But the road has been steep.

When we sat down at Janet's kitchen table and started talking about the idea for this book, we discussed our inspirations, our memories, and also our hopes for the future.

Here is Janet's story about her own path into politics:

> I wish I'd had a book like this when I was a kid.
>
> When I was a young girl, my mother and I went to the polls on Election Day to get signatures on a petition to ensure that all votes were counted equally. It was a cold day, but we got more than fifty signatures. Some years later, the Supreme Court decided that every vote should be equal. Everyone called it "One man, one vote" (even though it applied to women too!).
>
> I felt powerful. I felt I had made a difference.
>
> In college, I was fascinated by politics. I was a civil rights worker and participated in the 1963 March on Washington with Dr. Martin Luther King Jr., where again I felt that I could make a difference.

For almost fifteen years, I was a volunteer in my community. Slowly, it occurred to me that I should run for office, but there were so few women politicians that I wasn't sure it was even possible. In 1991, I took a chance and ran for a seat in the Virginia State Senate, where I have been ever since.

When we look at Theresa's daughters (Janet's granddaughters), we know they can thank the many women who stood up before them for the opportunities that may come their way. Recently, we have had the pleasure of seeing many more women get involved in politics and take on leadership roles. But we also know that women still have a long way to go — and that the final glass ceiling has yet to be broken, for our daughters and granddaughters and for all of us.

So here's to all of the women leaders from any party and all backgrounds who have stood up, stepped forward, and blazed trails. And here's to what's possible as women — and girls! — continue to lead us into the future.

— Virginia State Senator Janet Howell and Theresa Howell

A Guide to the Power Symbols

Integrity

★ Staying true to your beliefs
★ Speaking with honesty
★ Keeping to high standards
★ Ignoring criticism if necessary
★ Staying firm and playing fair
★ Passing the torch
★ Pitching in
★ Not letting others define you
★ Being yourself

Resourcefulness

★ Learning all the time
★ Keeping an open mind
★ Raising money for your cause
★ Thinking out of the box
★ Valuing intellectual creativity
★ Finding new solutions
★ Asking questions
★ Asking for help
★ Defying expectations

Community

★ Building a grassroots movement
★ Founding groups and clubs
★ Holding community meetings
★ Identifying and building a network of allies
★ Engaging powerful people
★ Seeking mentors and mentoring
★ Educating others
★ Organizing others
★ Bringing outsiders inside

★ Hard work
★ Harder work
★ Going the extra mile
★ Discipline
★ Leading by example
★ Planning
★ Preparation and rehearsal
★ Stepping up whenever needed

Diligence

How do powerful women leaders achieve their goals? What personal qualities help them along the way? Below are eight important character traits that great leaders often develop, along with some suggestions of how those qualities can be expressed. All of the women portrayed in this book have used each of the approaches at one time or another, but some women are true superstars when it comes to using certain tools. Look for the power symbols accompanying each portrait throughout the book. Which are your favorites?

Courage

- ★ Speaking truth to power
- ★ Protesting and boycotting
- ★ Taking risks
- ★ Standing up for your beliefs
- ★ Seizing opportunities
- ★ Embracing the role of underdog
- ★ Pushing through fear and discomfort
- ★ Volunteering for the hard stuff
- ★ Holding those in authority accountable

Empathy

- ★ Building bridges
- ★ Reaching out to diverse groups
- ★ Noticing who might be underrepresented
- ★ Using humor
- ★ Working face-to-face and seeking personal connection
- ★ Prioritizing inclusion
- ★ Being a good listener
- ★ Representing others well
- ★ Empowering and encouraging others

Persistence

- ★ Taking one step at a time
- ★ Never giving up
- ★ Patience
- ★ Turning negatives into positives
- ★ Seeing the long view
- ★ Fully engaging with each stage of the journey
- ★ Moving past defeat with grace and determination
- ★ Keeping your goal in mind

Communication

- ★ Giving speeches
- ★ Writing letters
- ★ Writing articles
- ★ Persuading others
- ★ Developing strong arguments and evidence
- ★ Speaking up
- ★ Creating posters and imagery
- ★ Making connections through social media

This woman's place is in the House . . . the House of Representatives!

BELLA ABZUG, also known as "Battling Bella," was a charismatic leader who fought fiercely and unapologetically for women's rights, first from outside the political realm and eventually from within, as a U.S. representative.

Bella liked to point out that she was born in 1920, the year women were finally able to vote in America. Her mother joked that Bella was born yelling. From a young age, Bella proved to be feisty and unafraid to take a stand on issues she felt were important. At twelve years old, she was giving speeches on the sidewalk outside her father's butcher shop in New York City about the need for a separate Jewish state. She even gave speeches on the subway in between stops and then asked the passengers for money for the cause. Bella also argued that girls should be able to play the boys' street games in her neighborhood if they wanted to, and she broke tradition in her synagogue by reciting a prayer that was meant to be recited strictly by men. When Bella wasn't advocating for social justice, she was learning Hebrew and studying music. She frequently got in trouble at school for being outspoken. In fact, in fourth grade Bella was disqualified from running for class president because she spoke out of turn. That didn't stop her. So many of her classmates wrote in her name on the ballot that she won anyway.

Bella's parents taught her that she could grow up to be whatever she wanted, and Bella decided early on that she wanted to be a lawyer. After graduating from college, she applied to Harvard Law School. "We take no females," Bella was told. Discouraged but undeterred, she went to Columbia Law School. At first, when Bella became a lawyer, clients assumed that because she was a woman, she was an assistant or a secretary, not a lawyer. It was then that she started her lifelong habit of wearing hats, believing it would lead people to take her more seriously. Hats became her trademark, but Bella made sure that people knew it was what was *under* the hat that mattered. As a lawyer, she focused on civil rights cases and also took on clients who were unfairly accused of being Communists by Joseph McCarthy, a U.S. senator who played on people's fears by suggesting, without evidence, that Soviet spies were embedded in the United States.

Eventually, Bella decided she wanted to be a part of writing laws instead of only defending them. She took the U.S. House of Representatives by storm in 1970, supporting causes that were controversial for the time and fighting for her right to wear a hat on the floor.

Bella spent her life speaking out for social justice, regardless of what people had to say. She wrote, "There are those who say I'm impatient, impetuous, uppity, rude, profane, brash, and overbearing. Whether I'm any of these things or all of them, you can decide for yourself. But whatever I am — and this ought to be made very clear at the outset — I am a very serious woman." Bella Abzug made a serious difference for women in this country.

BELLA ABZUG

1920–1998

U.S. REPRESENTATIVE FROM NEW YORK

> "**Women are not wedded to the policies of the past. We didn't craft them. They didn't let us.**"

I desire you would Remember the Ladies, and be more generous and favourable to them than your ancestors.

ABIGAIL ADAMS was born in 1744 in Weymouth, Massachusetts, during a time when America was still under British rule. She would go on to become one of America's Founding Mothers. As wife to John Adams, who became vice president and then president, she would serve as the Second Lady of the new nation, then First Lady. Throughout the American Revolution and the early days of the United

States, she was a trusted unofficial advisor to her husband, often representing a woman's perspective.

Abigail grew up in a small farming community as the daughter of a reverend. As a girl, she didn't have many options for her future. She was raised to take care of a home. She made candles and soap, gardened, sewed clothes, and made herbal medicines. She and her sisters did not attend school, but Abigail loved to learn. She was educated at home by her family members and the books they kept.

When Abigail was nineteen, she married John Adams, who was twenty-eight and a lawyer. He shared her love of books. John traveled a lot, and Abigail was often left on her own to manage the family farm and educate their children. During an outbreak of smallpox, she decided to have herself and her children inoculated against the disease — this in a time when vaccinations were new and not yet fully understood, yet were proving effective at protecting people from the highly contagious and often deadly disease.

In 1775, Abigail was appointed by the Massachusetts General Court to question the women in her community who did not support independence from Britain. John Adams proudly wrote to his wife, "You are a Politician, and now elected into an important Office, that of judgess of the Tory Ladies."

Abigail loved to write. During her lifetime, she wrote more than two thousand letters! Her letters provide a vivid account of the early days of our nation and show her as a woman with strong ideas about how to govern the country. She argued that girls should have an education equal to boys and that enslaved people should be freed.

Abigail Adams knew that, given the constraints on women in her day, she would never have an official say in making decisions about how the country would be run, but she wanted her voice to be heard. In her most famous letter, she wrote to her husband as the laws of the new nation were being formed: "Do not put such unlimited power into the hands of the Husbands. Remember all Men would be tyrants if they could. If particular care and attention is not paid to the Ladies we are determined to foment a Rebellion, and will not hold ourselves bound by any Laws in which we have no voice, or Representation." Those are brave words from a woman of her era. Unfortunately, the Founding Fathers didn't listen to her advice, but changes would come with time, and Abigail Adams would surely be proud to see what the women of her country have accomplished.

"I will never consent to have our sex considered in an inferior point of light."

IT TOOK ME QUITE A LONG TIME TO DEVELOP A VOICE, AND NOW THAT I HAVE IT, I AM NOT GOING TO BE SILENT.

MADELEINE ALBRIGHT was the first woman to serve as secretary of state to the United States. "I never expected to be who I am," she said. From being a war refugee as a child to working in the White House and representing the United States around the world as an adult, Albright has seen many twists and turns in her remarkable life.

Madeleine was born in 1937 in Czechoslovakia. When she was two years old, her family fled their country to escape the Nazis. They lived safely in England during World

War II, but Madeleine later learned that three of her grandparents had been killed in concentration camps during that time. Her family returned to Czechoslovakia only to have to flee again when the country was taken over by Communists. Madeleine was then eleven years old, and she still recalls the Statue of Liberty welcoming them as they arrived in America.

Growing up in New Jersey and Colorado, Madeleine tried hard to fit in. She learned to speak "American" without an accent, played field hockey, read comic books, and chewed gum like the other girls. In high school, she started an international relations club, named herself president, and held group discussions about international issues. Her friends remember her as being an intense person who took strong stands on issues she cared about.

Madeleine attended Wellesley College. There, she got her first taste of politics working as a volunteer for Adlai Stevenson's campaign for president. She attended rallies and collected money for the campaign on Boston Common, where she and other volunteers were threatened with arrest for soliciting money. She found the experience exhilarating.

Madeleine wanted to be a journalist, but once she got married, the expectation was that she would focus on her husband's career instead. On one occasion, a group of her husband's friends were discussing who among them would be the first on the cover of *Time* magazine. They asked Madeleine to get them something to drink while they talked about themselves. They never suspected that one day *she* would be the only one of them to be on the cover of *Time*.

While her kids were young, Albright earned her master's degree and PhD in public law and government. At the age of thirty-nine, she took her first government job, as chief legislative aide to Senator Edmund Muskie. She was then asked by her former professor Zbigniew Brzezinski to serve as legislative liaison for the National Security Council in the Carter White House.

In 1993, President Bill Clinton appointed Albright as ambassador to the United Nations. And in 1997, she became secretary of state, the chief advisor to the president on international affairs. She worked tirelessly in support of America's interests abroad and shone a light on women's issues in particular, saying, "The reason I made women's issues central to American foreign policy was . . . because we know that societies are more stable if women are politically and economically empowered."

Madeleine Albright is known for the vibrant brooches or pins she wears to express her mood, ideas, and sense of humor and to help break the ice with foreign leaders. She has always been a force to be reckoned with—assertive, straightforward, and a talented diplomat—and is still known for taking a definitive stand on what she believes.

> "Real leadership comes from the quiet nudging of an inner voice. It comes from realizing that the time has come to move beyond waiting to doing."

Don't listen to the naysayers and the cynics. There will be people who say you shouldn't, you can't, you won't. Just do it.

TAMMY BALDWIN is the first openly gay woman elected to Congress. She credits her success in politics to her willingness to take risks and her ability to shrug off discouraging comments from those who oppose her. "I thought I might have to make a choice," she has said. "Between pursuing a career of my dreams or being honest about who I am. Between public service and being myself in public. I decided I had to take my own risk."

Tammy was born in Madison, Wisconsin, in 1962. Her mother was only nineteen at the time and struggled with addiction, so Tammy's grandparents took her in and raised her. When Tammy was nine years old, she became ill and had to spend three months in the hospital. Her treatment and care were expensive, and her grandparents gave up a lot in order to afford it. It was an experience that would affect Tammy's outlook on health care and insurance for the rest of her life.

When she got involved with student government in middle school, Tammy experienced for the first time what it felt like to make a difference in her community. She and her fellow officers helped improve relations between the school and the neighborhood and raised money for a school in Nicaragua. It was empowering to see the effects of working together.

Tammy graduated from high school at the top of her class and went on to major in math and political science at Smith College, an all-women's school in New England, where she threw herself into campus life. During her junior year at Smith, Tammy began coming out as a lesbian, at first to those she was close to. She wanted to be honest with people about who she was even though she wasn't sure how revealing the truth would affect her future.

After graduation, she returned to Wisconsin to help take care of her grandmother and pursue her law degree at the University of Wisconsin. While in law school, at the age of twenty-four, Tammy was elected to the Dane County Board of Supervisors and briefly served on the Madison city council. During a discussion about whether to add a bus route, the men in the room argued that it was unnecessary, while the women pointed out that the new route was important for women taking night classes at a nearby school who didn't feel safe walking at night to the current bus stop. The board decided to add the new route.

TAMMY BALDWIN

1962–

WISCONSIN STATE REPRESENTATIVE

U.S. REPRESENTATIVE FROM WISCONSIN

U.S. SENATOR FROM WISCONSIN

> "Have faith in progress even when you cannot see it. Be the kind of leaders who inspire this faith in others."

After practicing law for a few years, Baldwin was elected to the Wisconsin State Assembly. She served three terms until she was elected to the U.S. House of Representatives, where she made history as Wisconsin's first congresswoman. As a U.S. representative, she advocated for universal health care, an issue of lifelong importance to her.

In 2012, Tammy Baldwin became the first openly gay person elected to the United States Senate. She noted that she didn't run to make history; she ran to make a difference. As a senator, she works toward improving health care, combating climate change, and securing LGBTQ rights. Her leadership demonstrates the power of sharing your own story and that you can both be yourself and run for office.

I am a believer in women and I believe in their possibilities.

MARY McLEOD BETHUNE was a social visionary. She fulfilled many roles in her life — educator, political leader, and the first black woman to head a federal agency — all with the goal of creating more opportunities and equality for black Americans.

Mary was born in 1875 in Mayesville, South Carolina, to two formerly enslaved people, Samuel and Patsy McIntosh McLeod. When Mary was born, there were no schools for black children in her community. Her sixteen brothers and sisters worked long days on their family's farm. But when Mary was ten years old, her world opened up because she learned to read. Her parents had decided to send one of their children to a new school for the children of former slaves, and they chose Mary. She woke up early, did chores, walked five miles to school, studied, walked home, did more chores, and then taught her siblings what she had learned at school.

Armed with an education, she began to dream. She had a vision that if black children, especially girls, were given equal access to education, they could accomplish great things and make a difference in America. In 1904, she opened a small school in Florida, where originally only five girls attended. They used smashed berries as ink and sat on furniture Mary made out of crates. Within two years, more than 250 children attended her school. It was said that Mary never turned a single child away. With hard work and the support of her community, her little school turned into a four-year college, still in existence today and now known as Bethune-Cookman University. Mary McLeod Bethune was its first president and the first black woman ever to be president of a college in America.

When women won the right to vote in the United States, Bethune went door-to-door to encourage black women to register to vote. This angered a white supremacist hate group known as the Ku Klux Klan. One day they surrounded her school and tried to intimidate Bethune and the children. She didn't back down. The Klan members left, and on Election Day, she and other black community members proudly voted and succeeded in electing the candidate of their choice.

Bethune became president of the National Association of Colored Women, a political group with more than ten thousand members that fought for equality for black women. When Franklin D. Roosevelt became president, he invited Bethune to the White House to give a report about the struggles young people were facing. She spoke passionately about the need to include consideration for black children in the administration's youth policies. She brought the president to tears. He appointed her to head a whole new department: the Division of Negro Affairs, within the National Youth Administration. Bethune was very influential in this position, and ultimately, a "Black Cabinet" was formed to advise the president and create policies.

Near the end of her life, she wrote, "I leave you love. . . . I leave you hope. . . . I leave you faith. . . . I leave you racial dignity." Her entire life, Mary McLeod Bethune faced and fought racism with intelligence and heart. Her work improved the lives of hundreds of thousands of Americans and helped pave the way for the civil rights movement and its legislative and social successes.

MARY McLEOD BETHUNE

1875–1955

DIRECTOR OF THE DIVISION OF NEGRO AFFAIRS

NATIONAL ADVISOR TO PRESIDENT FRANKLIN D. ROOSEVELT

"Our children must never lose their zeal for building a better world."

The die is cast—and all I can do is sit tight and take whatever of abuse or praise comes from such a blow to tradition.

HATTIE WYATT CARAWAY was the first woman elected to serve a full term in the U.S. Senate. She may not have started out with strong political ambitions, but the circumstances of her life led her to make a decision that would contribute to the progress of future women in leadership.

Hattie was born in 1878 near Bakerville, Tennessee. Her family had a farm and her father ran a general store in town, but Hattie always knew she wanted something else.

She was pretty sure that getting an education was the key to broadening her horizons. Her parents couldn't afford to send her to school, so she made a deal with her aunt: if she behaved well and got good grades, her aunt would pay for her schooling. She and her aunt both upheld the deal, and Hattie went to Dickson Normal School, a school that trained teachers.

After graduating, Hattie taught for a few years before marrying Thaddeus Caraway, a lawyer with an interest in politics. The couple had three sons and settled in Arkansas, where Hattie became involved with a women's club in town and was elected its secretary. In 1912, her husband was elected to Congress, and the family moved to Washington, D.C. With regret, Hattie had to give up her role in the club she loved so much. She began to focus on her husband's political life instead, helping with campaigning and acting as his personal advisor. In 1920, freshly granted the right to vote, Hattie cast the first ballot of her lifetime, voting for her husband, who was successful in his bid to become a U.S. senator from Arkansas.

In 1931, Thaddeus Caraway died unexpectedly. Wanting to maintain balance in the Senate, the governor of Arkansas appointed Hattie to hold her husband's seat. The expectation was that she would temporarily act as senator and vote as she thought he would have voted. Meanwhile, other men were being groomed to run for his seat in the upcoming election. A newspaper article stated, "Although she made no statement regarding the matter, leaders were confident that Mrs. Caraway would not seek to succeed herself in the next general election."

Surprise! That was not quite what Mrs. Caraway had in mind. "I really want to try out my own theory of a woman running for office," she wrote in her journal. Instead of stepping down when her husband's term ended, Hattie Caraway decided to run for his seat. This was *not* how things were normally done, but Caraway was steadfast, and when she won, she took her place in history as the first woman elected to the U.S. Senate for a full term.

In the Senate, Caraway was known as "Silent Hattie" because she so rarely spoke from the floor. Quiet though she was,

> **"The time has passed when a woman should be placed in a position and kept there only while someone else is being groomed for the job."**

Hattie Wyatt Caraway continued to make history as the first woman senator in many different ways, and she cast her votes with pride, often in support of programs that would help the people of Arkansas.

Hats off to Hattie, for helping to pave the way for more women in the Senate!

The affairs of the office of secretary of state were never in better order than under Mrs. Chacón's administration.

— Charles Coan

SOLEDAD CHÁVEZ CHACÓN

was the second woman and the first Latina in the United States to serve as governor, even if her tenure acting in that office lasted for only two weeks.

Soledad was born in 1890 in Albuquerque, New Mexico, to a middle-class Latino family. Not much is known of her childhood, except that she played both the piano and the mandolin. Her family had political roots, and they were proud of several of their ancestors who had been governors of New Mexico long ago. Soledad graduated from high school with honors and went on to graduate from the Albuquerque Business College with a degree in accounting. Both of these accomplishments were unusual for a woman at that time. Shortly after college, she got married and had two children. She was involved with a few different clubs in town: the Women's Club, El Club Latino, and a literary club.

One day, Chacón was at home baking a cake when five men came to her door. They asked if she would add her name to the ballot for secretary of state. Women had recently won the right to vote in New Mexico. The politicians currently in power were afraid that without a woman on the ballot, they'd lose the support of women voters. Once Chacón had the permission deemed necessary from her father and husband, she agreed to throw her hat in the ring. In 1922, she was elected secretary of state of New Mexico, making her the first Latina ever elected to statewide office in the United

States. One of the first things she did was to ask a female cousin to become assistant secretary of state. When her cousin turned down the position, Soledad's husband agreed to take the job.

> **"It is my earnest desire to carry out the plans and wishes of our governor during his absence, in as fearless and conscientious a manner as has been his policy."**

It was two years later that Soledad inadvertently made history once again. In 1924, the governor of New Mexico had plans to travel out of state in the summer. The lieutenant governor was slated to serve as acting governor during that time, but he died before the trip took place. Next in line to serve was the secretary of state — Soledad Chávez Chacón! The governor, with faith in her steady leadership, left the state of New Mexico in her hands. On her first day, she was greeted by lots of well-wishers. People realized that this was something new, something to remember. The newspapers reported that Chacón had taken over as acting governor, but focused more on her clothing and appearance than on her qualifications and accomplishments. During the two weeks that Chacón was in charge, she turned down a proposal that women with short hair should be required to tip their hats to women with long hair and also undertook several consequential initiatives, including petitioning for federal funds for New Mexico's National Guard. When the governor returned to New Mexico, Chacón returned to being secretary of state.

As a testament to her leadership, Chacón was elected some years later as the first Latina representative from Bernalillo County to serve in the New Mexico legislature. Her service was a sign that things were changing for women in America, albeit slowly. Soledad Chávez Chacón served with dignity and pride, and proved to those she worked with that she was a strong, capable leader.

If they don't give you a seat at the table, bring a folding chair.

SHIRLEY CHISHOLM was the first black woman elected to Congress. She called herself "Fighting Shirley Chisholm — Unbought and Unbossed," and she certainly lived up to that description.

Shirley was born in Brooklyn, New York, in 1924. During the Depression, when it was hard for Americans to find work, Shirley lived with her grandmother in Barbados.

When she returned to the United States, Shirley did well in school and impressed her teachers with her debating skills. While she was at Brooklyn College, one professor told her that she was a natural politician. Shirley was shocked. She knew of no black women in politics. Was that even a possibility? She became a preschool teacher instead, and then director of two local day-care centers. After she married Conrad Q. Chisholm, she went back to school for her master's degree in education.

The people around Shirley were drawn to her energy and her spirit. She was able to see clearly what needed to be fixed in her community, and she had ideas for how to change things. "You don't make progress by standing on the sidelines, whimpering and complaining," she said. "You make progress by implementing ideas."

In 1964, Shirley won a seat in the New York State Assembly, where she helped create benefits for domestic workers and college opportunities for disadvantaged students. In 1968, she ran for a seat in the U.S. House of Representatives. During her campaign, she won people over by talking to them face-to-face and listening to what mattered to them. Her fluency in Spanish helped her connect with Spanish speakers in her district. Because of her hard work and determination, Shirley Chisholm won the election and became the first black woman in Congress.

Shirley was a fiercely independent and self-confident person. She didn't always follow the rules because she felt that the rules weren't meant to help people in the margins. She wanted change. She wasn't afraid to speak her mind. She fought hard to combat discrimination against people of color, and she stood up for the rights of women and the poor. While in Congress, she helped found the Congressional Black Caucus, committed to addressing African Americans' concerns, and the Congressional Women's Caucus, dedicated to women's issues. She also worked passionately on issues such as education, assistance for school lunches, and extended hours for day-care centers.

In 1972, Chisholm ran for president of the United States as the candidate of the people. She campaigned all across the country, speaking out and bringing attention to issues important to her. She didn't win the Democratic nomination, but she helped smooth the path for more women to run for higher office.

Shirley Chisholm did things her own way and made a difference. She said, "I want history to remember me . . . not as the first black woman to have made a bid for the presidency of the United States, but as a black woman who lived in the twentieth century and who dared to be herself. I want to be remembered as a catalyst for change in America."

"**Tremendous amounts of talent are being lost to our society just because that talent wears a skirt.**"

To every little girl who dreams big: Yes, you can be anything you want— even president.

HILLARY RODHAM CLINTON won the popular vote for president of the United States in 2016, the first and only woman to have done so. Throughout her life, Clinton has achieved many firsts.

Hillary was born in Chicago in 1947 and grew up in Park Ridge, Illinois. From the time she was a small child, Hillary knew she wanted to be a leader. She was a Girl Scout and a safety guard, and she organized a mock Olympics in her neighborhood to raise money for charity. In high school, she played softball and was active with the

Young Republicans. When she ran for president of the student council and lost, she was told it was because there was no way a girl could win.

Hillary went to Wellesley College, an all-women's school in Massachusetts, and there was elected president of the student government. As the first student to give a speech at Wellesley's graduation ceremony, she stunned the crowd by outshining the senator who spoke before her. She received a seven-minute-long standing ovation. People were beginning to take notice of Hillary Rodham.

After she graduated, she spent the summer in Alaska, traveling, working as a dishwasher in Mount McKinley National Park, and sliming fish in a canning factory. After this adventure, she went on to Yale Law School, a different kind of adventure, where she focused on children's rights and where she met Bill Clinton, whom she later married. By this time, Clinton's political views had changed, and she aligned herself more with the Democratic Party.

Over the next twenty years, Clinton was busy professionally and with raising her daughter, Chelsea. She worked for the Children's Defense Fund, for the presidential campaign of Jimmy Carter, as a lawyer, and as a law professor at the University of Arkansas. When Bill Clinton was elected governor of Arkansas, Hillary became the First Lady of the state. That same year she also became the first female partner at the law firm where she worked.

In 1992, Bill Clinton was elected president of the United States, so the Clinton family moved into the White House. As First Lady of the United States, Hillary actively worked on health care reform and publicly advocated for women's and girls' rights around the world.

In 2000, Hillary was elected senator from the state of New York. She was the first former First Lady to serve in the U.S. Senate. While in office, she launched a rigorous campaign for president of the United States — another first for a former First Lady. In 2008, she lost the Democratic primary election to Barack Obama, who went on to become the first African American U.S. president.

President Obama knew that Clinton was a strong leader and appointed her as secretary of state. During her time in that post, she visited 112 countries, traveled more than one million miles, and worked with leaders from all over the world.

Never one to give up, Clinton ran again in 2016. This time, she became the first woman to win a major political party's nomination for president of the United States. She advanced to the general election and won the popular vote but ultimately lost the electoral college vote to Donald Trump. Hillary Rodham Clinton did not become the first woman president, but all the barriers she's broken down and the firsts she has achieved have made it easier for other women leaders to advance. In her concession speech, Clinton encouraged girls and women, saying, "I know we have still not shattered that highest and hardest glass ceiling, but someday someone will."

HILLARY RODHAM CLINTON

1947–

FIRST LADY OF ARKANSAS

FIRST LADY OF THE UNITED STATES

U.S. SENATOR FROM NEW YORK

U.S. SECRETARY OF STATE

FIRST FEMALE NOMINEE FOR PRESIDENT BY A MAJOR POLITICAL PARTY

"Human rights are women's rights — and women's rights are human rights."

Freedom empowers the heart. It levels walls and shatters ceilings, including glass ceilings.

ELIZABETH DOLE is the first woman to have held two different cabinet positions under two different presidents. On top of that, she served as the president of the American Red Cross and as a U.S. senator. She said, "Women share with men the need for personal success, even the taste for power. And no longer are we willing to satisfy those needs through the achievements of surrogates, whether husbands, children or merely role models."

Elizabeth was born in 1936 in Salisbury, North Carolina. As a child, she had a knack for organizing and leading things. She was elected president of her third-grade bird club, and in junior high school, she started her own book club and named herself its first president.

She went to Duke University, where she studied political science and was voted Leader of the Year by her classmates. After college, she enrolled in a joint education and government master's program at Harvard. Although she loved her time spent teaching, the government side of the program was where her passion lay. She sought the advice of Margaret Chase Smith, one of only two women in the U.S. Senate at the time, and Smith advised her to go on to law school. Elizabeth's mother, however, was not thrilled with her daughter's decision to attend Harvard Law School and asked if she wouldn't rather be a wife and mother instead. Not just yet, Elizabeth told her.

After earning her law degree, Elizabeth moved to Washington, D.C., and worked as a lawyer. She won her first case defending a man accused of annoying a lion at the zoo. She argued that since the lion wasn't there to testify, they couldn't rightly tell if it had been annoyed, now, could they?

Over time, Elizabeth held a number of high-level positions in government. During President Nixon's administration, she worked in the Office of Consumer Affairs and on the Federal Trade Commission. In 1975, she married Senator Bob Dole and temporarily quit her job to help him campaign when he was picked to run for vice president by President Gerald Ford.

> **"When you're in your nineties and looking back, it's not going to be how much money you made or how many awards you've won. It's really what did you stand for. Did you make a positive difference for people?"**

For the next twenty years, Elizabeth balanced working high-profile jobs and taking time off to help her husband with his multiple runs for president. President Ronald Reagan appointed her secretary of transportation; in that role, she helped change the legal drinking age to twenty-one and require air bags in new cars. As secretary of labor under President George H. W. Bush, she helped improve diversity and safety standards in the workplace. As the president of the American Red Cross, she led a major modernization of the organization's blood drive operations and strengthened its ability to respond to natural disasters.

Every once in a while, when Elizabeth was campaigning for her husband, people would tell her that *she* should run for president. In 1999, she did. Even though many people considered her the first serious female contender for president, she dropped out due to lack of funding. Two years later, she took a seat in the U.S. Senate, where she served with distinction.

Elizabeth Dole never was a First Lady or the first woman president, but she worked hard, made a difference, and transformed the role of women in politics with her achievements.

I HAVE TO . . . SHOW YOUNG GIRLS IN THIS COUNTRY THAT THEY TRULY CAN GROW UP TO BE WHATEVER THEY WANT TO BE.

TAMMY DUCKWORTH is an Iraq War veteran who has served as a U.S. representative and is currently a U.S. senator. "The lessons I learned as an officer," she wrote, "the challenges I've faced and the camaraderie I've experienced are at the core of who I am." She is the first Thai American woman to serve in Congress.

Tammy was born in Bangkok, Thailand, in 1968. When she was a child, her family moved all over the world because her father worked for the United Nations, helping refugees. When she was sixteen, they moved to Hawaii. Her family fell on hard times when her father lost his job, and they barely had enough money to buy food. To help her family, Tammy worked multiple part-time jobs after school, including selling flowers on the side of the road. She was a Girl Scout as well, which she has said taught her a lot about leadership.

Tammy studied political science in college and went on to graduate school, where she enrolled in the Army Reserve Officer Training Corps (ROTC). She became a commissioned officer in 1992 and was trained as a helicopter pilot. While she was working toward her doctorate in human services, she was deployed to Iraq. In 2004, her helicopter was hit by a rocket-propelled grenade. Duckworth lost both her legs and spent a year recovering at the Walter Reed Army Medical Center. She received several medals for her service, including a Purple Heart, and felt as if she had been given a second chance at life. Carrying on despite her injuries, she received a medical waiver to continue serving as a lieutenant colonel in the Illinois Army National Guard until retiring in 2014. Today, she has two titanium legs, one with an American flag printed on it and the other with a camo print. She learned to walk again and found new strength. "These legs are titanium. They don't buckle," she has said.

"It's important to have women in leadership positions, because our experiences are different from those of the men we serve with and that helps us identify problems we can fix."

After she recovered, Duckworth wanted to do something important with the rest of her life, so she became an activist for better health care for veterans. She found that people listened to what she had to say because of her experiences, so she ran for Congress. She lost, but she didn't give up. In 2009, President Barack Obama appointed her to the federal Department of Veterans Affairs, where she worked to help find housing and health care for veterans. In 2012, she ran for representative a second time and won. She was the first disabled woman ever elected to the U.S. House of Representatives. And in 2016, she ran for senator from Illinois and won.

Tammy Duckworth was the first senator to give birth while in office. Her baby daughter, Maile Pearl, has also achieved a first of her own: she was the first daughter to appear on the Senate floor while her mom voted. Talk about girl power!

No people can become first-class citizens unless they can speak for themselves.

CRYSTAL BIRD FAUSET was the first African American woman elected to a state legislature in the United States. She was a teacher, a political activist, a politician, and a true leader in the struggle to improve racial relations in America.

Crystal was born in 1894 in Princess Anne, Maryland. Her father was principal of Princess Anne Academy. When he died, Crystal's mother stepped up and took over as principal. Education was important to Crystal's parents. However, by the time she was five, both of her parents had died, and she and her siblings became orphans.

Crystal was sent to Boston to live with her aunt, who continued to emphasize education, just as Crystal's parents would have wanted. There Crystal attended integrated schools, with her eye on becoming a teacher one day.

After graduating from the Boston Normal School, Crystal worked as a teacher until a new and interesting opportunity came her way. In 1918, the Young Women's Christian Association (YWCA) started a program called the Girl Reserves. As field secretary, Crystal traveled around the country and set up clubs for African American girls, where they could exercise, learn new things, and strengthen bonds with one another. Some clubs named themselves after her, and Crystal Bird Clubs started popping up.

Crystal had a profound interest in putting an end to prejudice against black people in America. In 1927, she accepted a new challenge. With the American Friends Service Committee she set out to talk to as many people as possible in an attempt "to lift the curtain of misunderstanding" that was dividing black and white people in America. She gave hundreds of speeches, reaching tens of thousands of people. Sometimes she was encouraged by the progress she was making. Other times, she was saddened to see how deep the misunderstanding between people ran.

With a talent for teaching and the desire to reach even more people, Crystal went back to school and graduated from Teachers College at Columbia University. From there, she took her passion for creating bridges between people and fostering understanding to new heights. One way to reach a lot of people, she determined, was through politics. She got involved with various organizations and mobilized thousands of African American voters.

Crystal Bird Fauset was a woman who broke down barriers and charmed and inspired people. The Democratic Party took notice. They encouraged her to run for a seat in the Pennsylvania state legislature. In a district where the population was more than two-thirds white, during a time when racial tensions were especially high, Crystal won, making history in American politics. In office, she worked on legislation in support of better housing, better health, and better protections for working women. It wasn't long before she caught the attention of President Franklin Roosevelt and First Lady Eleanor Roosevelt, who invited her to work on programs for the benefit of all African Americans.

Crystal Bird Fauset worked as hard and as long as she could, never losing sight of her ultimate goal: to improve life for African Americans and to teach the world that all people deserve equal rights and freedoms regardless of the color of their skin.

"We should not want to think of America as a 'Melting Pot,' but as a great inter-racial laboratory where Americans can really begin to build the thing which the rest of the world feels that they stand for today, and that is real democracy."

DOORS HAVE OPENED. BARRIERS HAVE BROKEN DOWN. . . . BUT THERE IS SO MUCH MORE TO DO.

DIANNE FEINSTEIN is one of the longest-serving women in the U.S. Senate. She first went to Washington, D.C., in 1992, which was nicknamed Year of the Woman because more women entered into electoral politics that year than ever had before. An effective and hardworking leader, Feinstein has been in the Senate ever since.

Dianne was born in 1933 in San Francisco. Her father was a prominent surgeon who earned the respect of everyone he met. Her mother, on the other hand, was known to be erratic and to sometimes treat her children cruelly. Dianne developed a tough exterior in order to withstand her situation at home and would often ride her bike or horses for escape.

It was her uncle, Morris Goldman, who sparked her interest in politics. He took her with him to city council meetings, exposing her to the world of government. Dianne was transfixed. When she went to college, she jumped right into student government, where she got a taste of some of the ups and downs of the political process. During her campaign for vice president of the student council, Dianne was giving a speech at a fraternity house when one of the boys picked her up, tossed her in the shower with her clothes on, and turned on the water. She got drenched, but she didn't react in the moment. When she won the student council position, she had authority over fraternity party permits for the fall's big football weekend. That fraternity was denied its permit — until they apologized to her for the shower incident.

Dianne loved politics, and after college, she worked as an intern on city official George Reilly's ultimately unsuccessful campaign for mayor of San Francisco. She stayed up late into the night, working and learning about how campaigns are run. She also got married and had a daughter, although she and her husband soon divorced.

As a single mother, Dianne stayed involved in politics. She participated in civil rights protests and volunteered for political campaigns, including John F. Kennedy's. When she was given a job on a women's prison board, she had the opportunity to learn about the criminal justice system. Later, she also got married again.

Dianne Feinstein ran for office for the first time in 1969, winning a spot on the San Francisco board of supervisors. She rose to become the first female president of the board. Then tragedy struck. Two public officials in San Francisco, Mayor George Moscone and Supervisor Harvey Milk, were assassinated. Feinstein, right down the hall at the time, was the one who discovered Milk's body. As acting mayor, she steered the city through the aftermath of this shocking event. She subsequently served two terms as San Francisco's first female mayor. She ran for governor and lost, but she didn't give up. In 1992, she was elected to the U.S. Senate, where she has served for close to thirty years. During that time, she led the passage of a now-expired ban on assault weapons. Today, she continues on in the Senate as a strong and powerful voice on issues that matter to her.

DIANNE FEINSTEIN

1933–

MAYOR OF SAN FRANCISCO

U.S. SENATOR
FROM CALIFORNIA

"Heroism, I believe, is a trait that does not know race, color, creed, sex, or sexual orientation."

Some leaders are born women.

GERALDINE FERRARO was the first woman from a major political party to run for vice president. Even though she and presidential candidate Walter Mondale did not win the election, her nomination broke new ground for women.

Geraldine (known as Gerry) was born in 1935 in Newburgh, New York. Her father was an Italian immigrant, her mother a first-generation Italian American. When

Gerry was just eight years old, her father died unexpectedly, and it changed her life. Her family had to move, and her mother worked as a seamstress to support Gerry and her brother. Her mother believed that a good education was the key to becoming fully self-sufficient, so she sent her children to the best school she could afford.

One day, when Gerry asked her mom how to sew beads on dresses as she had watched her mother do so many times, her mother purposefully gave her the most difficult kind of beads to sew. Gerry couldn't do it. Her mother meant this as a lesson about how important it was to stay in school and study hard so she could get a dependable job. Gerry took the lesson seriously. Her grades were so good that she received a scholarship to Marymount College.

In college, Gerry edited the school newspaper and enjoyed playing sports. After college, she went to law school at night and worked as an elementary-school teacher during the day. She was one of only two women in her class and graduated with a law degree from Fordham University in 1960.

After she got married and had kids, she decided to stay at home to care for them when they were little. Still, she volunteered and got involved in local politics. Later, she was hired as an assistant district attorney for Queens County, New York, in charge of the special victims unit. The cases she worked on during that time made her want to get more involved in politics so she could make policies to help prevent crime and improve the lives of those affected by it. In 1978, an opportunity arose for her to run for Congress. She won and served in Washington, D.C., for three terms.

GERALDINE FERRARO

1935–2011

U.S. REPRESENTATIVE FROM NEW YORK

VICE PRESIDENTIAL CANDIDATE

U.S. AMBASSADOR TO THE UNITED NATIONS COMMISSION ON HUMAN RIGHTS

"We've chosen the path to equality. Don't let them turn us around."

In 1984, presidential candidate Walter Mondale chose her to join his ticket as his running mate. At the Democratic National Convention, when Geraldine Ferraro was announced as the party's first woman vice presidential nominee, the crowd went wild. "I stand before you to proclaim tonight: America is the land where dreams can come true for all of us," she said in her acceptance speech. The campaign was difficult, and they lost to the incumbent, Ronald Reagan. But Ferraro's candidacy was an inspiration for many women.

After the election, she continued her work in public service. She ran twice for a seat in the Senate, losing both times, but served during the Clinton administration as U.S. ambassador to the United Nations Commission on Human Rights. Through her vice presidential run, Geraldine Ferraro had already made history, showing women that they could aspire to even the highest levels of leadership.

Being ladylike does not require silence.

BETTY FORD was the First Lady of the United States from 1974 to 1977. She emerged as an advocate for issues concerning women, such as equal pay, breast cancer, and addiction. Ford's honesty and openness helped to create awareness about matters that were previously difficult for Americans to discuss.

Betty was born in 1918 in Chicago, Illinois. Her father was a traveling sales-man, so her family moved around a lot, until they eventually settled down in Grand Rapids, Michigan. Growing up, Betty loved playing hockey and football with her older brothers. In seventh and eighth grades, she played on an all-girls football team that competed against the boys' teams and often won. Her true passion, though, was dance. Betty took lessons for years and got her first job at age fourteen as a dance instructor for little kids. Additionally, she and her mother were volunteers with the Mary Free Bed Guild, a rehabilitation hospital in Grand Rapids. Betty organized dance parties for the children at the hospital, joyful experiences for all.

After high school, Betty moved to New York City to study under the famous dancer Martha Graham. She loved the experience, but when she didn't make the travel troupe, she returned home. After marrying William Warren in 1942, she worked as a dance instructor and as a fashion coordinator at a department store. Her marriage was an unhappy one, however, and after five years together, the couple divorced. Then Betty met Gerald Ford, a lawyer with an interest in politics. They were married in 1948, two weeks before Ford was elected for the first time as a U.S. representative from Michigan. Betty and Gerald had four children, and during the time she was raising her kids, Betty chose to keep a low profile and stayed out of the public eye.

Then history took an unexpected turn. When Vice President Spiro Agnew resigned his post over corruption charges, President Richard Nixon appointed Gerald Ford to take his place. Then in 1974, facing impending impeachment over the Watergate scandal, President Nixon resigned. According to the U.S. Constitution, Gerald Ford was now president of the United States.

Nobody had ever seen a First Lady like Betty Ford before. She referred to herself as First Mama, wore a mood ring, and danced through the halls of the White House. More importantly, she spoke openly and honestly about things that had been considered taboo for a First Lady to talk about. While in the White House, she was diagnosed with breast cancer. Instead of hiding her struggle, she used the experience to raise awareness about the disease. She spoke out for women's rights, even when some in her husband's administration would have preferred her to be quiet. She led marches and gave speeches in support of the Equal Rights Amendment, which would guarantee equal rights for men and women in America.

Gerald Ford ran for president in 1976 and lost, but Betty Ford would perhaps have the most influence on American culture after his presidency was over. In 1978, her family confronted her about her addiction to alcohol and pills. At first, she resisted what they had to say, but eventually she agreed that she needed help. After her recovery, Betty once again went public with her private struggles. She established the Betty Ford Center to help treat others struggling with addiction, making sure that women were treated with the same care and regard as men. Betty Ford was unafraid to show the world her true self, and as a result, she opened the door for Americans to face reality, seek treatment, and improve the quality of their lives.

"The long road to equality rests on achievements of women and men in altering how women are treated in every area of everyday life."

So often in life, things that you regard as an impediment turn out to be great good fortune.

RUTH BADER GINSBURG is a Supreme Court justice known as a strong, independent thinker who is unafraid to dissent.

Ruth was born in Brooklyn, New York, in 1933. She was a bright, hardworking student with a mind of her own. "My mother told me to be a lady. And for her, that meant be your own person, be independent," she has said. Ruth's mother died the day before Ruth's high-school graduation, but Ruth has always kept her mother's words close to her heart.

She went on to Cornell University, where she met Martin Ginsburg, the love of her life. They were married after she graduated, then moved to Oklahoma, where Martin served in the U.S. Army. Ruth worked at a local Social Security Administration office. When she told her employer she was pregnant with her first child, she was demoted. Frustrated by this act of sexism, Ruth enrolled at Harvard Law School when her husband's military service ended. In a class of five hundred students, she was one of only nine women. Some men accused her of taking a man's spot in the class, but she knew she had a right to be there.

After moving to New York with her young family, Ruth transferred to Columbia Law School and graduated at the top of her class. Despite her academic credentials, she was turned down for many jobs just because she was a woman, which seemed highly unfair to her. Eventually, she was hired as a professor at Rutgers Law School in 1963. At that time, she was only the nineteenth woman law professor in the whole country. And there were thousands of laws on the books that discriminated against women.

Because of her experiences in school and in the workplace, Ruth devoted her life to fighting for gender equality. In 1972, she cofounded the Women's Rights Project at the American Civil Liberties Union. As the director of this program, she argued several cases in front of the Supreme Court, brilliantly choosing some in which a man was the victim of a gender-based law to show that discrimination on the basis of sex was not fair to either gender. The rulings of the cases she argued brought attention to the negative consequences of treating men and women differently and pushed America toward more fair and balanced laws.

> **"People ask me sometimes, When will there be enough women on the court? And my answer is when there are nine."**

In 1980, President Jimmy Carter appointed her to the U.S. Court of Appeals for Washington, D.C. Thirteen years later, President Bill Clinton appointed her to the Supreme Court of the United States, making her the first Jewish woman to serve on the court.

Now in her eighties, Ruth Bader Ginsburg continues on strong, even pursuing a regular workout routine (including twenty push-ups!). On the bench, she has made a name for herself with her well-thought-out opinions and her steadfast belief in equality for all. "I try to teach through my opinions, through my speeches, how wrong it is to judge people on the basis of what they look like, color of their skin, whether they're men or women," she has said.

THE GOVERNORSHIP IS NEITHER A MAN'S NOR WOMAN'S WORK. I SEE IT AS A PEOPLE'S JOB.

ELLA T. GRASSO was the first woman in America elected as governor without succeeding her husband. "I realized that if I was concerned with problems, the best way of getting them solved was to be part of the decision-making process," she said.

Ella was born in 1919 in Windsor Locks, Connecticut. Her parents had moved from Italy to America to find work in Connecticut's textile mills. Ella grew up surrounded by a close-knit community of family and friends. Her father started a bakery in town, a popular place for locals to gather and talk. Her mother was known as a woman with strong political opinions; she had very little education, but she loved to read and always kept up with the news. Regular household talk about current events is what first sparked Ella's interest in politics.

Ella's grades were so good that she got a scholarship to a private all-girls school nearby. She had to learn to straddle two different worlds once she entered school: the wealthy, privileged world of her school and the working-class world of her hometown. It was a skill she used throughout her political career. Ella was able to relate to almost anybody. Very few women from Ella's town went to college, but Ella did. She went with the support of her family and a scholarship.

After she graduated with a master's degree in economics, she got involved with the League of Women Voters, a nonpartisan group dedicated to educating and registering women to vote. When Ella learned that her town didn't have a local chapter of the League, she founded one.

In 1952, Ella Grasso won a seat in the Connecticut House of Representatives, where she fought for equal rights and against housing discrimination. Leading Democrats noticed that Grasso's policies and leadership style appealed to both men and women, and her background as a daughter of immigrants helped give voice to the many immigrants in her state. In 1958, she was elected the secretary of state of Connecticut. In addition to her official duties in this role, she traveled all over the state, giving speeches and listening to people. In 1970, Grasso threw her hat into the ring for a seat in the U.S. House of Representatives. With an already impressive track record of

> **"I urge you to seek roles that are meaningful — that will make you active participants in the important events of the day."**

winning elections, Grasso won again. She served for four years but deeply missed Connecticut, so she set up what came to be known as the Ellaphone, a direct line for Connecticut residents to call to express their opinions and concerns.

In 1974, Grasso ran for governor of Connecticut and won. She governed with charisma. Instead of riding in the governor's limo, she chose to drive her own small blue car. When the Blizzard of 1978 dumped thirty inches of snow on Connecticut, she shut down all roads and businesses and took a hands-on approach to dealing with the matter. Her strong, supportive leadership during the crisis earned her the nickname Mother Ella.

Ella T. Grasso had to resign from the governorship during her second term because she was gravely ill, but, beloved by many, she left her post with the knowledge that she had made a difference.

ELLA T. GRASSO

1919–1981

CONNECTICUT STATE REPRESENTATIVE

SECRETARY OF STATE OF CONNECTICUT

U.S. REPRESENTATIVE FROM CONNECTICUT

GOVERNOR OF CONNECTICUT

Push through the fear.

NIKKI HALEY served as the United States ambassador to the United Nations, and before that, the governor of South Carolina. She wrote, "When the daughter of Indian immigrants, who grew up in a small rural town in the segregated South, can become the first female and minority governor of her state and the youngest governor in the nation, then it's clear that the American Dream still exists."

Nikki was born in 1972 in Bamberg, South Carolina. Hers was the only Indian American family in the whole town. Nikki loved her small community, but she had to learn to stand up to bullies. She found refuge at Girl Scout camp, being part of a diverse group of girls with different religions and backgrounds who didn't judge one another and had fun together. At twelve years old, Nikki started working in her mother's women's clothing store, which would eventually grow to become a major company. She wrote checks, did the taxes, and made sure that all of the store's finances were in order. It was a big job for a kid, but she learned that she was really good at working with numbers.

At Clemson University, she studied accounting. She loved the friendly, diverse community at college and the feeling of belonging. When she returned to work for her mother's company, she found she was able to inspire women employees to use their voices and make a difference. She also helped the company to grow significantly, began to serve on local chambers of commerce, and in 2004 became president of the National Association of Women Business Owners.

That same year, Nikki decided to enter a race for a seat in the South Carolina House of Representatives. Many people thought she had no chance of winning. Nikki Haley shocked everyone when she won against the longest-serving legislator in South Carolina.

Eventually, she decided to run for governor of her state. Again, she was considered the underdog, but she didn't let that stop her. Haley came from behind and surprised people with a strong win. As governor, she started an anti-bullying program. Partly due to her experiences when she was young, she wanted to take action to protect kids from bullying.

When, in 2015, there was a tragic, racially motivated shooting of nine worshippers at the Emanuel African Methodist Episcopal Church in Charleston, Haley took a stand that led to the removal of the Confederate flag from the state capitol grounds.

In 2016, Nikki Haley was nominated by President Donald Trump to be the U.S. ambassador to the United Nations. She was sworn in in January 2017 and served through 2018. "I love this country," she has said. "And when you are given an opportunity to help your country, in what is one of the most volatile times we've seen in a long time, there's no way I'm not going to step up to do everything I can and make us strong."

> "I hope that women continue to find the power of their voice. Because I do think if women ran the world, we would have true peace and security."

I am sick and tired of being sick and tired.

FANNIE LOU HAMER was a national political leader and a courageous woman devoted to fighting for the rights and well-being of African Americans at any cost.

Fannie Lou was born in 1917 in Montgomery County, Mississippi. Her family were tenant sharecroppers. As kids, she and her nineteen brothers and sisters helped their parents in the fields. Fannie Lou could pick more than one hundred pounds of cotton a day, but because her family had to hand over such a large amount of their crop to pay for the land they lived on, it was difficult for them to make enough to feed and clothe themselves. Fannie Lou noticed the difference between how white and black people lived in Mississippi and knew it wasn't fair. Her mother was a strong woman who protected her children and tried to bring joy into their difficult lives. She taught her daughter to respect herself so that others would respect her as well.

When Fannie Lou Hamer was forty-four years old, she went to a meeting and learned that she, and all African American citizens, had the right to vote. This fact had been hidden from Hamer her whole life because white people in the South did not want black people to vote. Empowered by this knowledge, Hamer went to register to vote right away. But it wasn't that easy.

At the county offices, she learned that in order to register to vote, black citizens first had to take a test. Nearly impossible to pass, this test was a tactic deliberately used by white officials to deny African Americans their voting rights. Hamer returned home, still unable to vote, and later lost her job because of her attempt to register. She wasn't intimidated. Instead, she was even more determined to exercise her right to vote and to help others exercise theirs as well. It was dangerous work. Some who tried had their homes burned down, lost their jobs, saw their families threatened, or even lost their lives.

Hamer understood the risk. She traveled around the South for the cause of freedom and equality. Once, after sitting at a whites-only lunch counter in South Carolina, she was arrested. In jail, she was beaten so badly that it affected her health and vision for the rest of her life. But that did not stop her. Not at all. She just got more determined. She helped to start a new political party that spoke to the concerns

FANNIE LOU HAMER

1917–1977

CIVIL RIGHTS ACTIVIST

COFOUNDER AND VICE CHAIR OF THE FREEDOM DEMOCRATIC PARTY

COFOUNDER OF THE NATIONAL WOMEN'S POLITICAL CAUCUS

> "So whether you're white, black, or polka dot, we made from the same blood, brother, and we are on our way."

of African Americans. It was called the Mississippi Freedom Democratic Party. And she ran for Congress, knowing that her candidacy would bring attention to the issues that mattered to her and inspire more African Americans in Mississippi to register to vote.

In 1964, Hamer spoke at the Democratic National Convention. She told her story and exposed the truth about the racist discrimination in Mississippi. Her speech was broadcast on televisions across America and is considered one of the most important speeches given during the civil rights movement because of the bitter truths it described and the emotion with which she delivered it.

In 1971, Fannie Lou Hamer, along with others such as Bella Abzug, Shirley Chisholm, and Gloria Steinem, helped to found the National Women's Political Caucus to help increase the number of women running for office. She was steadfast in her fight against the oppression her people were made to suffer. She stood tall and refused to be silenced. She was a beacon of hope and an American hero.

The American dream belongs to all of us.

KAMALA HARRIS is a U.S. senator from California — the first American senator in history of South Asian descent and the first black senator for California. "My mother had a saying," Harris has commented. "'Kamala, you may be the first to do many things, but make sure you're not the last.'"

Kamala was born in 1964 in Oakland, California. Her mother was from India and her father was from Jamaica. They were both active in the civil rights movement in the 1960s in Berkeley, California, giving Kamala a "stroller-eye view" of the fight for racial equality in the United States. When she was a child, she got to travel regularly to Jamaica and India; in both places, she was further inspired by the conversations and activism of her family members abroad. After her parents divorced, she and her sister were mostly raised by their mother, who had very high expectations for her girls. They helped clean test tubes in their mother's science lab, sang in the church choir, and learned to cook Indian food. When Kamala was thirteen years old, she organized a protest at the building she and her family lived in because children weren't allowed to play soccer on the lawn. The protest was successful, and before long, the neighborhood kids were playing soccer in the building's green space.

After high school, Kamala went to Howard University, one of the nation's premier historically black colleges, where she ran for student council, participated in the debate team, loved to dance, and started a mentoring program for minority kids. After graduating, she pursued a law degree at the University of California, Hastings, and then went on to work for the San Francisco district attorney's office. She ran for district attorney of San Francisco, and in winning became the district's first woman, first black American, and first South Asian American to be elected to the position.

As a prosecutor, Harris developed a reputation for being fearless and tough on crime. She wanted to be a voice for vulnerable people. Her accomplishments as a lawyer and her ideas about how to prevent crime helped her to win the election to become California's attorney general, a position she held for six years.

Then, in 2016, she jumped into a race for a seat in the United States Senate. She won, and has been considered a leader in her party since then, unafraid to speak up and take a stand for what she feels is right. She serves on several high-profile committees, including the Senate Judiciary Committee and the Committee on Homeland Security and Government Affairs. She works for civil and women's rights and advocates for students.

In almost every position she has held, Kamala Harris has represented a first of one kind or another. Taking to heart what her mother taught her about making sure she won't be the last, she makes time to mentor women seeking public office because she believes more women are needed in all areas of government. In 2019, she declared her candidacy for the presidency of the United States.

KAMALA HARRIS

1964–

DISTRICT ATTORNEY OF SAN FRANCISCO

ATTORNEY GENERAL OF CALIFORNIA

U.S. SENATOR FROM CALIFORNIA

PRESIDENTIAL CANDIDATE

"Women have an equal stake in our future and should have an equal voice in our politics."

If my life has any meaning at all, it is that those who start as outcasts may end up being part of the system.

PATRICIA ROBERTS HARRIS was the first black woman to

become a U.S. ambassador and the first black woman to serve as a U.S. cabinet secretary. Driven to work for social justice, she made history along the way.

Patricia was born in 1924 in Mattoon, Illinois. When she was six years old, her parents divorced, and from then on Patricia was raised by her mother. Strong, capable, and smart, her mother was her first and most important inspiration and taught Patricia to be independent and steadfast in her opinions. Patricia loved to read. She read out loud to her grandmother and devoured whole series of books on her own time. By high school, Patricia and her family had moved to Chicago, where she kept her nose in books and her eye on college.

Patricia was offered a scholarship to Howard University, in Washington, D.C. At Howard, she was as studious as ever but also got involved with civil rights activism long before the civil rights movement was in full swing. Angered that segregation was a way of life in the capital of the United States, Patricia led a group of her fellow students in a sit-in protest against a diner near the school that refused to serve black people. Every five minutes, a student walked into the restaurant and requested service. When it was denied, they sat down, occupying a seat, until the whole place was filled with protesters. Within days, the diner reversed its policy on whom they would serve and the students claimed victory. Patricia graduated with a degree in political science and economics and continued working for civil rights.

Years later, she wanted to take the fight for civil liberties to the courtroom. Her husband, William Beasley Harris, seeing what she was capable of, encouraged her to pursue her dream and go to law school. She graduated first in her class at George Washington University Law School and got involved in the Democratic Party, where her leadership skills were noticed by President Lyndon B. Johnson. He appointed her as U.S. ambassador to Luxembourg, making her the first African American woman to hold this rank. When she accepted the position, she said, "I feel deeply proud and grateful this president chose me to knock down this barrier, but also a little sad about being the 'first Negro woman' because it implies we were not considered before."

That wasn't her only first. Harris eventually became the dean of Howard Law, making her the first African American woman to be dean of a law school. Always open to new experiences, she later decided to put her law degree to use and worked at a major law firm.

In 1977, President Jimmy Carter appointed Harris as secretary of housing and urban development. During her confirmation hearings, she explained that she was suited for the position not only because of her education and accomplishments, but also because of her early experiences with poverty. She understood the sting of discrimination. In 1980, also under President Carter, she became the first-ever secretary of health and human services. In her history-making roles, Patricia Roberts Harris protected civil and women's rights by supporting social programs, appointing women and people of color to important posts, and helping revive troubled neighborhoods. After serving at the federal level, Harris ran for mayor of Washington, D.C. When she lost, she returned to teaching. Always a reader, she filled her home with books and a lifetime of memorabilia from her accomplishments as a woman who fought injustice and broke down barriers wherever she could.

> "While there may be others who forget what it meant to be excluded from the dining rooms of this very building, I shall never forget it."

REMEMBER THIS IS YOUR TIME. THIS IS YOUR HISTORY TO BE MADE.

CARLA HAYDEN is the first woman and first African American to serve as Librarian of Congress. In this role, she serves as the head of the Library of Congress, in Washington, D.C., the largest library in the world.

Carla was born in 1952 in Tallahassee, Florida. She spent the first ten years of her life living in Queens, New York, and moved to Chicago with her mother after her parents got divorced. Reading was always an important part of Carla's life. Her parents were musicians, and though she didn't follow in their footsteps musically, she felt like the words on a page coming alive in her mind had a voice of their own. The book that made the biggest difference for her as a child was a picture book called *Bright April* by Marguerite de Angeli, about an African American Girl Scout facing racial prejudice and making new friendships. Carla saw herself reflected in the pages of that book and has never forgotten the importance of feeling represented in literature.

After Carla graduated from Roosevelt University with a degree in political science and African history, she got a job as a children's librarian at the Chicago Public Library. She loved it and decided that librarianship was what she wanted to pursue for her career. While continuing to work, she went back to school and received both her master's and doctorate degrees in library science from the University of Chicago Graduate Library School. Hayden then taught at the University of Pittsburgh School of Information Sciences until she moved back to Illinois to take a position as chief librarian at the Chicago Public Library. At that time, she became acquainted with fellow Chicago residents Michelle and Barack Obama.

In 1993, Hayden was appointed as the director of the public library system in Baltimore, Maryland, which is made up of twenty-two libraries and is known overall as the Enoch Pratt Free Library. She sees libraries as important places where people can come together, access information, use the internet, and enhance their lives. She focused on making Enoch Pratt relevant in a time when libraries were changing from places to check out books to fully functioning community centers. In 2015, when the city of Baltimore was experiencing unrest after one of its residents died in police custody, Hayden made sure to keep the library in the center of the turmoil open. Neighbors found refuge, food, community, and solace within the walls of their library.

In 2003 and 2004, as president of the American Library Association, Hayden was a strong defender of personal privacy during a time when the government wanted libraries to hand over information about the books patrons were checking out and the internet searches they made. She fought to keep users' records private.

> **"As a descendant of people who were denied the right to read, to now have the opportunity to serve and lead the institution that is the national symbol of knowledge is a historic moment."**

In 2016, Carla Hayden was sworn in as American's fourteenth Librarian of Congress. The Library of Congress houses more than 168 million items, including millions of books, the largest comic book collection in the world, sheet music and musical instruments, and items such as a life mask of Abraham Lincoln and Rosa Parks's recipe for peanut butter pancakes. It's America's library, and as America's librarian, Hayden wants to make the incredible wealth of history and information held in the Library of Congress accessible to as many people as possible.

I've been a fighter all my life. I just don't look like that.

MAZIE HIRONO is the first Asian American woman elected to the U.S. Senate, the first woman senator from Hawaii, and the first U.S. senator born in Japan.

Mazie was born in 1947 in Fukushima, Japan. Her childhood was hard. Her father was an alcoholic and a gambler who left the family when Mazie was still small. Her mother, determined to make a better life for her family, boarded a ship with her children and sailed to the United States. In Hawaii, Mazie lived in a crowded boardinghouse with other immigrants. Her mother held two jobs, and Mazie helped to earn money for their basic needs by working as a lunchroom cashier and delivering newspapers. No one in the family spoke English at first, but Mazie loved listening to her school's librarian read aloud, and with time she learned the new language and ended up graduating from high school with honors.

Mazie's experiences as a child made her want to help people facing similar challenges when she was older, and that goal has been a guiding force throughout her life. She worked her way through college, also making time to volunteer at a mental-health facility, and then moved on to Georgetown University Law Center.

Hirono was electrified by the political climate in the 1960s. Protests against the war in Vietnam were popping up all over the country. Women were taking a stand and demanding equal treatment in the workplace and at home. It was then that Hirono knew she wanted to step up and lend her voice to causes she believed in. She began by running the campaigns of candidates who supported causes she cared about before she ran herself. Once she got her start as a politician, she steadily rose through the ranks. In 1980, she won a seat in the Hawaii House of Representatives. In 1994, she was elected as lieutenant governor of Hawaii. She suffered a setback when she lost her election for governor, but she quickly got back on her feet. In 2006, she was elected to the U.S. House of Representatives, and then, in 2012, to the U.S. Senate.

All the while, she has fought for the things she holds to be important, with families and children at the top of her list. When she was young and her family had very little financial stability and no health insurance, her greatest fear was that her mother would get sick and be unable to work. As a senator, Hirono herself was diagnosed with cancer. Luckily, she received the treatment she needed, but she never forgot what it felt like to be without necessary resources. She gave a passionate speech on the Senate floor about how important it is that all Americans are able to get the health care they need so they don't have to live in fear of getting sick.

Today, Mazie Hirono is known as a senator who speaks her mind. She has said, "I am a woman, I am a minority person, and I speak in a very plain way. And I think that reaches people."

MAZIE HIRONO

1947–

HAWAII STATE REPRESENTATIVE

LIEUTENANT GOVERNOR OF HAWAII

U.S. REPRESENTATIVE FROM HAWAII

U.S. SENATOR FROM HAWAII

"If I had to wait around for somebody to pick me . . . I never would have been picked."

These types of positions do not come overnight but with a lot of time, concentration, hard work.

DIANE HUMETEWA is the first Native American woman to serve as a federal judge. She is an important role model for Native American students across the country who dream of one day serving on the country's highest courts.

Diane was born in 1964 as an enrolled member of the Hopi tribe, one of the oldest cultures in North America. Growing up, she split her time between two very different worlds: the Hopi reservation — an expanse of land in Arizona spotted with mesas, buttes, rock art, and sage — and the city of Phoenix. On the reservation, Diane hauled water in buckets up to her grandmother's house, which had only one faucet and no electricity. Because Diane's father worked for the Bureau of Indian Affairs, she got to travel throughout Arizona's Indian Country. When her parents were children, they had been forced to leave their families and attend government boarding schools, where they would be punished if they practiced Hopi traditions. Diane's parents didn't want that for their own children, so they enrolled their kids in the Phoenix public schools, hoping that would give them an advantage in life and help them learn to successfully navigate both cultures.

DIANE HUMETEWA

1964–

**U.S. ATTORNEY
FOR ARIZONA**

**U.S. DISTRICT JUDGE
FOR ARIZONA**

Diane was the first person in her family to go to college, thanks to the encouragement of her parents. She was interested in teaching and working with young people, but she wasn't sure what she wanted to do for a career. When she got a job working with the federal courts in Arizona, she developed a passion for supporting the victims of crime, especially those from Indian Country. Lawyers saw the innovative work she was doing and told her she should consider law school.

Humetewa enrolled at Arizona State University's Sandra Day O'Connor School of Law with the Indian Legal Program so she could better understand law as it relates to Native peoples. During her second year, she applied for an internship in Washington, D.C., with Senator John McCain. This opportunity and the support she received from the professors and mentors in her law program taught her that her opinions mattered and that she could have a bright future.

After she graduated, she accepted an offer from Senator McCain to work on the Senate Indian Affairs Committee. Today, Diane Humetewa is considered an expert on issues unique to Indian Country. In 2007, she was appointed as the first Native American woman U.S. attorney. She was humbled and honestly surprised to learn

**"It is a proud moment for her, her tribe, and for Native Americans."
— John McCain**

that in the year 2007, she was the only Native woman in her position. In 2013, President Barack Obama nominated her to serve as a U.S. district judge. She was confirmed with a rare unanimous vote. Her parents proudly watched the vote take place from their home in the Hopi Nation.

There is a great need for more Native people to be represented in the American judicial system. Judge Diane Humetewa receives letters and emails from people all over the country expressing their support of her accomplishments. In turn, she works to improve higher education among tribal members so that in the future a Native American federal judge won't seem so rare.

I BELIEVE AMERICA IS THE BEST PLACE IN THE WORLD TO BE A WOMAN.

KAY BAILEY HUTCHISON didn't know she wanted to be involved in politics until she was an adult, but once she dipped her toe in, she was captivated. She has had an exciting career as a politician in many different capacities.

Kay was born outside Galveston, Texas, in 1943. A top student and a Girl Scout, Kay also studied ballet and performed with the Houston Youth Symphony Ballet. On top of that, one summer when she was around ten years old, she got the idea to start a camp for the kids in her neighborhood, and her mother supported her. They held the camp in their home, and each day Kay developed activities to entertain the kids who came.

After graduating from college, Kay didn't want to do what most of the other graduating women were doing, which was getting married or teaching. She went to law school instead. There she thrived. When she tried to get a job after graduation, though, she was told time and time again that this firm or that just couldn't hire a woman. After one particularly frustrating interview, Kay went into a local television station and inquired about a job as a news reporter. The station had never hired a woman for that position, but they liked Kay's energy and the fact that she had a law degree. Suddenly, Kay was on television every night, covering Texas politics. That was how she got introduced to politics and where her interest in governing began.

KAY BAILEY HUTCHISON

1943–

TEXAS STATE REPRESENTATIVE

TEXAS STATE TREASURER

U.S. SENATOR FROM TEXAS

U.S. PERMANENT REPRESENTATIVE TO THE NORTH ATLANTIC TREATY ORGANIZATION (NATO)

Because of her job as a reporter, Kay became familiar with all the goings-on in the Texas legislature. Before long, she decided to run for office herself. And she won. In 1973, she began serving as the first Republican woman in the Texas House of Representatives. After two terms, she shifted to the U.S. National Transportation Safety Board. Then she took a break from politics. During that time, she worked in banking, and she bought her own candy company. How sweet is that? But the call of politics still rang in her ear. In 1990, she won the election for Texas state treasurer. And in 1993, she won a seat in the United States Senate, making her

"Like most women, the way I've gotten ahead is by working harder than most men are willing to work."

the first woman to become a U.S. senator from Texas. She was a successful senator, always busy serving on several committees, always working hard. To Kay, it's important to have a mix of men and women serving in government. She has worked on many ideas in support of women that she feels would have been totally overlooked if women weren't in the Senate to point out how important they were.

Today, because of her extensive experience in military affairs and defense spending, Kay Bailey Hutchison serves as the permanent representative to the North Atlantic Treaty Organization (NATO). "I've had to fight for everything I get," she has said. She works hard and has managed to turn the few failures in her life into giant successes, and that's what we call grit.

The greatest motivation . . . has to come from inside you.

BARBARA JORDAN was the first southern black woman elected to the House of Representatives. She was a smart, savvy, determined woman who played an important role in American politics.

Barbara was born in 1936 in Houston, Texas. Her father, a preacher, ran a strict household. She and her sisters weren't allowed to go to the movies or to dances. Her parents expected their children to get excellent grades, dress properly, speak well, and show respect. Barbara loved spending time with her grandfather, who taught her to be proud of herself and to love the color of her skin. Barbara went to a segregated school in Houston. In school and in church, she was known for her strong and booming voice. She loved to sing and talk. Sometimes she even got in trouble at school for talking too much. Then she discovered the debate team, the perfect place for a girl with a talent for talking.

Barbara knew she wanted to do something special in her life; she just wasn't sure what. In high school, she heard a speech given by an inspiring black female lawyer. Right then, Barbara decided that she also wanted to be a lawyer. Getting there took a lot of work. She went to Texas Southern University, then to Boston University School of Law. At law school, she was one of only six women, and one of only three women of color, in her entering class. Barbara began to see how the segregated school she had attended in Texas was not equal to the schools her white classmates had gone to. So she stayed up late every night, studying and catching up. Law school was difficult, but she learned a lot and came to firmly believe that segregation was a bad policy.

Barbara graduated and passed the bar exam. When she returned to Texas, she opened her own law practice. Inspired by politics, she volunteered for John F. Kennedy's presidential campaign. Even after he won, she continued to give speeches, encouraging people to register to vote. Segregated schools still bothered Barbara, so she cofounded a group called People for Upgraded Schools in Houston. PUSH, as it was called, organized a citywide boycott of the Houston schools. On the day of the event, students walked out of school in the middle of the day and marched peacefully to the school board building. Shortly afterward, due to her efforts, a new law was passed requiring Houston schools to be integrated.

"We must provide the people with a vision of the future."

When Barbara decided to run for office, she was told not to bother. But racism, or even the promise of racism to come in the election, didn't stop her. She ran for state senator, won, and served two terms. In 1972, she won a seat in the U.S. House of Representatives. There, she played a key role in the decision to move toward impeaching President Richard Nixon. In 1976, she gave the keynote address at the Democratic National Convention—the first woman and the first black person ever to do so. "My presence here," she said in her booming voice, "is one additional bit of evidence that the American Dream need not forever be deferred."

Later in life, her health declined and she needed a wheelchair to get around. But that didn't stop her either. She was one of the most popular teachers at the University of Texas and continued to lead and give speeches. Barbara Jordan was awarded the Presidential Medal of Freedom in 1994, a testament to her status as an American hero.

I don't think my position unusual for a woman. I'm following a perfectly natural urge to do what I like.

CLARE BOOTHE LUCE was a journalist, a playwright, a U.S. congresswoman, and the U.S. ambassador to both Italy and Brazil. She was witty, with supreme confidence and the determination to live life as large as she possibly could.

Clare was born in 1903 in New York City. Her mother was a former chorus girl and her father a traveling violinist. They moved so often that Clare and her brother didn't have the chance to enroll in school. Instead, their dad taught them to read and provided them with books whenever he could. When her father left the family,

Clare's mother untruthfully told the kids he had died. Faced with surviving on her own, Clare's mom became fixated on making Clare a movie star. While Clare had a few stints onstage and in front of a camera, that dream never came to be, but one day in the future, she would become a player on the national stage. Although Clare's early schooling was sporadic, she read fervently to catch up and became a brilliant student with dreams of becoming a writer.

Clare was full of energy and big hopes when she got involved with the women's movement. In 1919, she was hired as the young public face of the movement, tasked with recruiting new members to the cause. But when she met millionaire George Brokaw, she changed directions and got married. They had one daughter, but it was an unhappy marriage, and they later got divorced.

After the divorce, Clare wanted to revive her dream of being a writer and asked the publisher of *Vogue* for a job at the magazine. He said no, but Clare showed up anyway and started writing captions for photos until he gave in and let her stay. In no time, Clare was the managing editor of *Vanity Fair,* where she helped shift the focus of the magazine to politics. Immersed in the magazine world, Clare met and married Henry Luce, the publisher of *Time, Life,* and *Fortune* magazines. Clare's play *The Women* premiered in 1936, with a film to follow in 1939.

Because of her involvement with the country's most-read magazines, Clare had a platform to express her opinions about politics. She had strong conservative opinions and a national voice as a journalist. She also worked as a war correspondent during World War II and witnessed some of the war's atrocities firsthand. When she decided to run for Congress in 1942, she won and became the first woman elected to Congress from Connecticut. She used her knowledge of foreign affairs to guide her but often had to combat the prejudiced view that women were not capable of functioning in politics. She planned to run for the Senate and maybe even the vice presidency, but everything changed when her only daughter was killed in a car accident. Clare Boothe Luce was elected for a second term but chose not to run for a third.

In 1953, Clare reentered politics when she was confirmed as the U.S. ambassador to Italy, the first woman ever appointed to a major ambassadorial post. Several years later, she was confirmed as the U.S. ambassador to Brazil. In both roles, she represented the United States' interests and negotiated with world leaders.

Impossible to ignore, Clare Boothe Luce barged right into what was considered a man's world at the time and forged her own path, making way for a new world of possibilities.

CLARE BOOTHE LUCE

1903–1987

JOURNALIST

U.S. REPRESENTATIVE FROM CONNECTICUT

U.S. AMBASSADOR TO ITALY

U.S. AMBASSADOR TO BRAZIL

> "If I fail, no one will say, 'She doesn't have what it takes.' They will say, 'Women don't have what it takes.'"

No one told me there were limitations. Of course, I would not have listened to them if they had tried.

WILMA MANKILLER was the first woman ever elected principal chief of the Cherokee Nation. "Prior to my becoming chief, young Cherokee girls never thought they might be able to grow up and become chief themselves," she said.

Wilma, the sixth of eleven children, was born in 1945 in Tahlequah, Oklahoma, the capital of the Cherokee Nation. For his growing family, her father built a four-room house, lit with coal-oil lamps and heated by a wood-burning stove. The Mankillers used the cold spring nearby for water and to refrigerate their food. Wilma's connection with her people was strong. She attended traditional Cherokee ceremonies, and her life was filled with stories. From these, she learned that her family's last name, Mankiller, traditionally referred to the person in charge of protecting the community. She learned about the Trail of Tears, the deadly atrocity caused by the U.S. government's forcing thousands of Cherokee people to leave their homeland and travel over twelve hundred miles on foot to live in an unfamiliar place.

When Wilma was ten, her family experienced an unwanted relocation of their own. As part of the Indian Relocation Act, the government offered to pay Cherokees to move away from their homes on the reservation to start a new life in cities around the country. Wilma's family moved to San Francisco, and she was miserable there. Kids made fun of her name, her accent, and her clothes. She did not feel at home in the city and lost nearly all of her self-confidence. Wilma found comfort and community at San Francisco's Indian Center. Being an outsider eventually taught Wilma to be tough, and with the love and support of her family, she learned to accept herself and be proud of who she was.

In 1969, Wilma participated in the occupation of Alcatraz Island, in San Francisco Bay. The demonstration was intended to show that Alcatraz belonged to Native Americans before the United States took it away. After this experience, she knew that she wanted to spend her life fighting against injustices suffered by Native Americans.

Mankiller returned to Oklahoma with her two daughters and just twenty dollars in her pocket, but at last she felt as though she was home. When she started working for the Cherokee Nation of Oklahoma, she was invigorated. But then she was involved in a terrible car accident. Relying on her toughness, Mankiller recovered and took courses in community planning. She worked as a community developer to accomplish things that no one thought possible, like bringing clean water into a community that had no plumbing. She focused not only on bringing people what they needed, but on inspiring them to get things done themselves.

Mankiller never considered campaigning for office until the chief of the Cherokee Nation asked her to be his running mate. He had seen what she was capable of and knew she'd be a strong candidate. Wilma was so surprised that at first she said no. Eventually she accepted and, after a tough race, became the first female deputy chief of the Cherokee Nation.

By the next election, she had decided to run for chief. She set out to challenge the stereotypes of what a woman could do. As chief, she inspired people to feel personal pride and to be the leaders in their own lives. During her tenure, membership in the Cherokee tribe doubled! Wilma Mankiller was indeed a protector of her people.

> **"The most important issue we have as a people is [to] believe in ourselves enough to . . . articulate our own vision of the future."**

GROWING UP, I NEVER IMAGINED A LITTLE GIRL FROM A BORDER TOWN COULD ONE DAY BECOME A GOVERNOR. BUT THIS IS AMERICA. EN AMÉRICA TODO ES POSIBLE.

SUSANA MARTINEZ was the first female governor elected in the state of New Mexico and the first Latina governor ever elected in the United States.

Susana was born in 1959 in El Paso, Texas. By the time she was five years old, she had earned the nickname la abogada, which in Spanish means "the lawyer," because she frequently questioned and tried to negotiate rules with her parents. She was first exposed to politics helping her father campaign for candidates her family supported.

She and her dad canvassed their neighborhood and stuffed envelopes with campaign literature. In high school, she was a cheerleader and senior class president. She was raised to put family first and has always been a fierce advocate and devoted caregiver to her developmentally disabled sister, Leticia. She also worked for her parents' security guard business. At age eighteen, Susana wore a uniform and carried a gun when she guarded the parking lot during church bingo games.

Susana remembers watching politicians on the news and wondering how they got to be there. She didn't know whom to ask, but she figured out on her own that many of them were lawyers. With her eye on politics, she decided to pursue a law degree and become a real-life abogada. She studied criminal justice at the University of Texas at El Paso, then continued on to the University of Oklahoma College of Law. During law school, when asked about her career goal, Martinez replied that she hoped to be the first woman president of the United States.

After she graduated, Martinez worked as an assistant district attorney in Doña Ana County, New Mexico, choosing to focus mainly on cases that involved women and children. She said she was less interested in blazing a trail as a Latina and more interested in blazing a trail working to help victims of abuse. Martinez was raised as a Democrat, but when she got older, she realized her views were more aligned with the Republican platform. In 1996, she was elected district attorney, beating out her former boss for the position. As district attorney, she continued bringing legal action against criminals and was named New Mexico Prosecutor of the Year.

Hoping to take on a leadership role and bring change to her state's government, Martinez ran for governor of New Mexico in 2010. With the support of some leaders of the Republican Party, she won first in 2010 and again in 2014. During her time in office, Governor Martinez worked alongside Democrats and Republicans to balance the budget and improve standards in education. She has been a leader during natural disasters such as fires and droughts. Martinez was viewed as a rising political star, and there was some discussion about whether she might be Mitt Romney's vice presidential running mate in 2012, but she insisted that she would not be interested in the position because she wanted to focus on New Mexico and stay near her sister. After serving two terms as governor, Martinez reached her term limit.

Does she still want to be America's first woman president? For now, she is caring for her family, including her sister, but is proud to have been a role model for future politicians. Talking about how girls in her state often recognize her, she said, "It's in moments like these when I'm reminded that we each pave a path. And for me, it's about paving a path for those little girls to follow. They need to know—no more barriers."

"Challenges shouldn't scare us. They should inspire us to step forward and prove equal to the task."

I can't change the past, but I can certainly help somebody else in the future.

PATSY TAKEMOTO MINK was the first woman of color and the first Asian American elected to Congress. She was a determined, outspoken person who lived her life trying to create equality for all in America.

Patsy was born in 1927 in Paia, Hawaii. She grew up surrounded by sugarcane plantations and the people who worked there, in the time when Hawaii was a territory of the United States, not yet a state. When Patsy was a teenager, the Japanese bombed

Pearl Harbor, in Hawaii. Afterward, because her family was Japanese American, they faced discrimination and suspicion. They had absolutely nothing to do with Japan's actions during World War II, but people treated them differently.

Patsy was class president and valedictorian of her class at Maui High School. She had a way of uniting the different groups of students in her school. She was interested in becoming a doctor, so she went to the University of Hawaii and studied chemistry and zoology. She joined the debate team and was elected president of the premedical students club.

Patsy transferred to the University of Nebraska and was immediately upset by racially discriminatory practices she noticed at the school. She took action and formed a coalition of students who wanted to make the university fair and equal for all students. By the time she left and largely due to her efforts, the school had changed its policies, desegregating fraternities, sororities, and dormitories. After graduating, Patsy wanted to go to medical school, but despite her accomplishments as an undergraduate, she was rejected by all of the schools she applied to. She later learned that the rejections came because she was a woman.

Eventually, she chose to go to the University of Chicago Law School. After she graduated, though, no law firms would hire her, for the same reason. She opened up her own law practice and became Hawaii's first Japanese American woman lawyer.

Patsy decided to get involved in politics so she could work to change laws she considered unfair. She served in the Hawaii Territorial Legislature and then the Hawaii State Senate before she ran for the U.S. House of Representatives, broke down all the barriers before her, and won.

While in Congress, Patsy Mink accomplished her goal of creating more equality between men and women. She coauthored the Title IX Amendment to the Higher Education Act, which has made a huge difference for women in America. Imagine if there were no women's sports in college, and very few in high school. Imagine getting turned away from a field of study just because you were a girl. According to Title IX, "No person in the United States shall, on the basis of sex, be excluded from participation in, be denied the benefits of, or be subjected to discrimination under any educational program or activity receiving Federal financial assistance." Those words have opened the doors to new opportunities for women in the United States to play sports, participate in school programs, and hold the careers they dream of.

Patsy Mink served in Congress for twelve terms over the course of several decades. She ran for president in 1972 but didn't win. She said, "I've run many, many times, and I've lost many times, but I've never given up a feeling that I, as an individual, and you, as an individual, can make the difference." Patsy Takemoto Mink definitely made a difference.

PATSY TAKEMOTO MINK

1927–2002

HAWAII TERRITORIAL REPRESENTATIVE

HAWAII STATE SENATOR

U.S. REPRESENTATIVE FROM HAWAII

PRESIDENTIAL CANDIDATE

"Women's rights are about fundamental justice."

WHEN WOMEN RUN FOR OFFICE, WHEN PEOPLE OF COLOR RUN, WE OPEN UP THE POSSIBILITY THAT WOMEN AND PEOPLE OF COLOR CAN WIN.

CAROL MOSELEY BRAUN was the first black woman elected to the U.S. Senate. She held a number of political positions that led her all the way to a presidential run. Moseley Braun has said that "the most important thing we can do for our children, all of them, boys and girls, is to lead by example and to show them that in this country our notions of equality and fairness apply to everybody."

Carol was born in 1947 in Chicago, Illinois. From an early age, she knew she learned differently from others. She had a hard time matching the sound of a letter to what it looked like on the page. Although her dyslexia made it difficult for her to read, Carol knew she was smart. Determined to prove the teachers who thought otherwise wrong, Carol developed a way to read using a ruler to keep the words lined up on the page. Eventually, she was considered one of the smartest students in her class. Learning to deal with dyslexia taught Carol the value of hard work and to see connections where others did not.

Carol learned about politics by watching her father, a police officer and community activist. While working to desegregate their neighborhood schools, he showed her that if there's something you're unhappy about, you need to step up and try to fix it. Carol took that lesson to heart and staged some protests of her own. As a teenager, when she and a friend walked along a beach in an attempt to desegregate it, people threw stones at them. And once, she went to a diner in an all-white neighborhood and sat there for over an hour while the staff refused to serve her. When, finally, a waitress brought her a cup of coffee, Carol paid for it and left without taking a single sip. She also marched for civil rights with Dr. Martin Luther King Jr. in Chicago's Gage Park.

Carol's first year of college at the University of Illinois was difficult, so she took some time off. When she returned, she jumped back in and participated in student government. She earned her degree in political science and went on to get her law degree. She married in 1973 and worked as a U.S. attorney before taking some time off after she had a baby.

"My late mother used to say it doesn't matter if you came to this country on the *Mayflower* or a slave ship, through Ellis Island or across the Rio Grande. We're all in the same boat now."

One day, while she was out walking with her son, she had a conversation with someone who encouraged her to run for an open seat in the Illinois House of Representatives. Some thought that she, as a black woman, had no chance to win, so she decided to see for herself. She did win. Then, in 1992, she ran for the U.S. Senate. She was elected in what became known as the Year of the Woman because more new women were elected that year than ever before. As a U.S. senator, Carol Moseley Braun worked for women's issues and civil rights. She also focused on education, never forgetting her experiences as a bright young student with special needs.

In 1999, she became the U.S. ambassador to New Zealand and Samoa, and in the 2004 election cycle, she was a candidate for the Democratic nomination for president. "I ran for president largely because my ten-year-old niece called me in and showed me her social studies book and said, 'Auntie Carol . . . all the presidents are boys.' Well, I wanted her to know that presidents didn't necessarily have to be boys. Presidents could be girls, too."

THEY'LL TELL YOU YOU'RE TOO LOUD, THAT YOU NEED TO WAIT YOUR TURN AND ASK THE RIGHT PEOPLE FOR PERMISSION. DO IT ANYWAY.

ALEXANDRIA OCASIO-CORTEZ is the youngest woman ever elected to Congress. "Women like me aren't supposed to run for office," she said. But she ran, all right, and she won, signaling a change in the tide of politics. She was twenty-nine when she was elected.

Alexandria was born in 1989 in New York City. Her father, an architect from the Bronx, met her mother in Puerto Rico. Even from a young age, Alexandria, a Girl Scout, showed political gumption. Her family often talked about politics around the dinner table, and she was not afraid to chime in with her opinions, even if they differed from everyone else's. In high school, she loved science and won second place in an international science and engineering fair. In recognition of that achievement, an asteroid was named after her: the 23238 Ocasio-Cortez. Talk about a rising star!

Alexandria first got a taste of what running for office might be like when she participated in the National Hispanic Institute's Youth Legislative Session, a program geared toward future leaders and one she still supports today. Alexandria went to Boston University, where she studied economics and international relations. During her sophomore year, her father died. Alexandria dealt with the difficult loss by throwing herself into her studies. Following her interest in politics, she also started working for Senator Ted Kennedy on immigration issues.

She returned to the Bronx after graduation to help her mother and work on issues that were important to her, including early literacy and education. She started a children's book company with a focus on stories set in the Bronx. She taught summer classes on community leadership. When it looked like her mom might lose their home, Alexandria worked as a waitress to supplement the income her mother earned from cleaning houses and driving a bus. She sometimes worked more than eighteen hours a day but still made time for community meetings and local politics. The experience of struggling to keep her home and afford health care led her to get involved in national politics. In 2016, she volunteered for Senator Bernie Sanders's presidential campaign as an organizer. After that, Alexandria felt moved to talk with people around the country about the struggles they endure and the ways they survive, so she hopped in a car with two friends and visited places like Flint, Michigan; Standing Rock, in North Dakota; and Ohio. She listened to the stories people had to tell and walked away feeling that despite their differences, many Americans share common goals and ideals.

When she returned to New York, she started thinking about running for political office — something she had never before considered, something she never thought she'd have a chance at. She decided that even though the odds might be against her, she should still try. She started by meeting with people in their homes for coffee parties and having conversations about what mattered to them. She worked hard to register new voters and get community members involved in her campaign.

"I am running for Congress," she wrote, "because not caring is not an option anymore. Change is up to us, and it's up to you. Don't let anyone trick you into believing you need to be more than who you are in this moment. You are enough to pursue your dreams." By winning, and by her strong public presence since taking office, including her vocal sponsorship of the idea of a Green New Deal, Alexandria Ocasio-Cortez has demonstrated for the world that if we work hard enough, each of us can make a difference.

ALEXANDRIA OCASIO-CORTEZ

1989–

U.S. REPRESENTATIVE FROM NEW YORK

"In my opinion, if women and gender-expanding people want to run for office we can't knock on anybody's doors; we have to build our own house."

The power I exert on the court depends on the power of my arguments, not on my gender.

SANDRA DAY O'CONNOR was the first woman to serve as a justice on the United States Supreme Court. When she was sworn in, she broke the 192-year streak of only men serving as justices on the country's highest court.

Sandra was born in 1930 in El Paso, Texas. Her parents owned the Lazy B Ranch in

Arizona, where Sandra helped with ranch chores. By the time she was eight years old, she could ride horses, drive tractors, and mend fences. She was a real cowgirl! During the school year, she lived with her grandmother in Texas, where she did well in school and enjoyed playing tennis. She graduated two years early from high school and was accepted to Stanford University at the age of sixteen.

After graduating from law school at Stanford, she married John Jay O'Connor and began to look for ways to put her law degree to work. She was shocked at how difficult it was to find a job. Most law firms at that time didn't hire women, simply because they were women. When the O'Connors had their first son, Sandra and a friend started their own law firm — one with friendly, flexible conditions for mothers.

After some time off, and when her sons were a little older, O'Connor got involved in politics. She worked for the attorney general's office in Arizona and volunteered for political causes. She became an Arizona state senator and soon the majority leader of the Arizona State Senate, the first woman to ever be the majority leader of any state senate. It was an honor, but she missed practicing law. She became a judge and was appointed to the Arizona Court of Appeals.

In 1981, President Ronald Reagan nominated Sandra Day O'Connor for the Supreme Court. She was confirmed unanimously by the Senate. As a Supreme Court justice, Sandra was known to be fair but firm. She made an effort to decide each case based on the law and the Constitution without letting her personal opinions affect her decisions. She felt responsible for proving that women could do the job of Supreme Court justice, and she showed the world that she could do it very, very well. Some even referred to her as one of the most influential people in America. "Freedom and equality are not achieved overnight," she wrote. "Democracy takes work and time and constant effort."

> "Liberty requires us to place ourselves in another's shoes, to see that things may not be as fair or as equitable as they appear from our own vantage points."

Justice Sandra Day O'Connor retired from the Supreme Court in 2006 at the age of seventy-five. In 2009, President Obama presented her with the Presidential Medal of Freedom.

GET INVOLVED, FOR THE FUTURE — FOR YOUR CHILDREN AND GRANDCHILDREN. FOR WOMEN AND GIRLS.

NANCY PELOSI became Speaker of the House of Representatives for the first time in 2007, attaining the highest political office of any woman in the history of the United States. Known as Madam Speaker, she took control of the U.S. House of Representatives, gavel and all.

Nancy was born in Baltimore, Maryland, in 1940 to a political family. Her father was a congressman and then mayor of Baltimore. The first time she saw the Capitol, in Washington, D.C., was at her father's swearing-in ceremony. She thought it was the most beautiful building in the world. Her mother took an active role as First Lady of Baltimore, helping to run campaigns and speaking out for better housing in their community. From her, Nancy learned that women could be active participants in politics. When Nancy was in high school, her mother allowed her to attend an event with special guest John F. Kennedy, the most inspiring political figure of the time. Somebody took her picture with Kennedy, who was then a senator. Nancy didn't know that she herself would run for office decades later, but today that photo can be found in her office on Capitol Hill.

While attending Trinity College, in Washington, D.C., Nancy met her future husband, Paul. Together, they had five kids within six years. The family lived in San Francisco, where Nancy enjoyed the work of raising her children. She ran carpools, cooked meals, and sewed Halloween costumes. She also got involved with the Democratic Party as a volunteer: helping with campaigns, stuffing envelopes, and making phone calls, often involving her children in her activities. She rose to become chair of the California Democratic Party. Later, when she ran for chair of the Democratic National Committee, she lost. She has said that this loss helped her learn how to accept defeat. She followed the advice "Organize, don't agonize" and moved on.

When most of her children were grown, Pelosi became interested in running for political office. She thought the skills she had learned as a mother could help her in politics. In 1987, her family, including all of her kids, encouraged her to run in a special election for a seat in Congress. She won, and she has been in Congress ever since.

Using her political acumen, she rose to become the House minority whip and then House minority leader — the first woman to hold either of these posts. In 2007, she became Speaker of the House, a role she held for two consecutive terms. Pelosi is a strong advocate for more

> "**Know your power. When you do, others will know your power, too.**"

women in roles of leadership. She believes it's important for women to understand that they are powerful. Upon taking the oath of office in 2007, Pelosi said, "We have made history. Now let us make progress," and she immediately got to work.

In 2019, Nancy Pelosi again took over the gavel for the second time and a third term when her party regained control of the House after the midterm elections of 2018. She was the first person to regain the powerful role of speaker in over sixty years.

Feminism means revolution, and I am a revolutionist.

FRANCES PERKINS was the first woman to serve as a cabinet member in the United States government. President Franklin D. Roosevelt appointed her U.S. secretary of labor, a position in which she helped create a number of historically significant programs that we still benefit from today.

Frances was born in 1880 in Boston, Massachusetts. Although her father never went to college, he loved to read and started teaching Frances Greek when she was eight years old. He also fostered and fully supported his daughter's ambition to go to college. At Mount Holyoke, a women's college, Frances took the hardest classes because, even if she didn't always get the best grades, she felt that the challenge built character. She majored in chemistry, an unusual choice for women in her day but one that would allow her to be a science teacher for a time after college. During her senior year, something happened that had a great impact on her. For a class assignment, she toured local factories and reported on the working conditions there. She was shocked by what she saw. Women and children were forced to work extremely long hours without restroom breaks in unsanitary and dangerous factories — or else risk being fired.

Frances was moved to do something about what she had seen. After college, she ran a girls' club — a place for female factory workers to get exercise and services. When one of the workers lost a hand due to an accident on the job, Frances pushed to get her much-needed help. And with that, Frances's quest for a career with purpose had begun. She volunteered in the settlement houses of Chicago, where education, food, and services were provided to those in the neighborhood and where everyone, regardless of race, religion, or gender, was welcome.

After receiving her graduate degree in economics and sociology from Columbia University, Frances started an investigation into the working conditions of the bakeries in New York City. Again, she was appalled by what she learned. Then, in 1911, she witnessed the tragic fire at the Triangle Shirtwaist factory in New York, where 146 workers died, and she knew she had to do something. A commission was formed to study factory conditions, and Frances was one of the chief investigators. She forced the leaders of the commission to actually *see* what was going on, dragging them around to factories where small children worked and where fire escapes were broken and dangerous. This resulted in real change: new laws were enacted to improve conditions for working people.

> **"I had a kind of duty to other women to walk in and sit down on the chair that was offered, and so establish the right of others long hence and far distant in geography to sit in the high seats."**

Frances met Franklin D. Roosevelt while she was living in New York. He was well aware of the good work she was doing, so when he became president, he appointed her secretary of labor. During her long tenure in the position, she helped institute Social Security, end child labor, and secure a forty-hour workweek. Even though she met with resistance, she advocated on behalf of Jewish refugees seeking asylum during World War II, including devising a plan to allow hundreds of Jewish children to come to the United States. She improved lives, and she saved lives.

Frances Perkins was an outspoken, independent woman with creative ideas for improving conditions for the working people of America. She had to fight sexism, but she persisted, and America is a better place for workers because of her leadership.

Men and women are like right and left hands; it doesn't make sense not to use both.

JEANNETTE RANKIN was the first woman elected to Congress. "I may be the first woman member of Congress, but I won't be the last," she declared. And right she was!

Jeannette was born near Missoula, Montana, in 1880. During that time, women weren't allowed to vote. After college, Jeannette was restless. She tried teaching and dressmaking before becoming a social worker, helping immigrant families. She wanted to see better working conditions for women and better care for mothers and children. Most of all, she was frustrated that women had no say in elections. So she joined the women's suffrage movement and fought for women's right to vote by organizing people around the cause, hanging posters, and giving impassioned speeches.

In 1914, non-Native women in Montana won that right. Two years later, Jeannette Rankin ran for a seat in the U.S. House of Representatives, vowing to work toward securing the right to vote for all American women. In 1916, she made history when she was elected to go to Washington, D.C., to represent Montana in Congress.

JEANNETTE RANKIN

1880–1973

U.S. REPRESENTATIVE FROM MONTANA

Rankin was a woman who stood up for what she believed in whether people liked it or not. She believed that for America to be a true democracy, women across the country needed the right to vote. She was also a champion for peace, believing that if more women were in charge, there would be less violence in the world.

Rankin kept her vow to fight for women's suffrage. She argued for a special committee dedicated to women's right to vote. As the first congresswoman and a member of the committee, she spoke out in support of a constitutional amendment to extend suffrage for all women. Her efforts helped to advance the cause, but women across the country would have to wait a few years more.

"We're half the people; we should be half the Congress."

During her first term in Congress, Rankin, a pacifist, voted against going to war with Germany in World War I. More than twenty years later, she was elected to Congress a second time. Again, she was asked to vote on a war. But her arguments against fighting were ignored. She was told to sit down when she expressed her opposition to entering World War II. She voted no anyway because she felt strongly that war was the wrong way to solve any conflict. As a consequence, Rankin was booed and hissed at on the floor of Congress. After the vote, she had to hide in a telephone booth from reporters and angry bystanders. But she remained steadfast in her beliefs.

Although she didn't win reelection, Rankin continued to work for peace for the rest of her life. When she was eighty-seven years old, she led a march in Washington to protest the Vietnam War. "You can no more win a war than you can win an earthquake," she said.

Jeannette Rankin opened the door for women everywhere to run for Congress—and to vote their conscience.

In America, with education and hard work, it really does not matter where you came from — it matters where you are going.

CONDOLEEZZA RICE was the first black woman to serve as secretary of state for the United States. "Don't let anyone determine what your horizons are going to be," she has said. "You get to determine those yourself." With the support of her family, Condoleezza decided to set her horizons far and wide.

Condoleezza was born in 1954 in Birmingham, Alabama, during a time when segregation was enforced and racial tensions were high. When she was a child, black people weren't allowed to go to the same schools, eat at the same restaurants, or even drink from the same water fountains as white people. But her parents taught her how to stand up for herself and be proud. Once, when Condoleezza and her mother were shopping, Condoleezza was told to use the back storage closet to try on a dress instead of the whites-only dressing room. Her mother said they wouldn't spend their money in a store like that, and eventually the clerk gave in. Her family also believed that a good education was the way to a bright future. Condoleezza studied French, piano, and ballet. She loved sports, especially football.

In college, Condoleezza became fascinated by Russia and international politics. She learned everything she possibly could and went on to earn a PhD in political science from the University of Denver. All the while, she stayed active in sports. She played tennis and golf and was a competitive ice-skater. She believes sports are a great way to develop leadership skills because of the hard work and cooperation required to succeed. She used her expertise in international affairs and became a very popular political science professor at Stanford University. She taught her students to follow their passion but to try things outside of their comfort zones too.

Rice developed a reputation through her writings as an expert in Russian affairs and culture. Rice first went to Washington, D.C., in 1986, to serve as a special assistant to the Joint Chiefs of Staff. She next worked as President George H. W. Bush's chief advisor on the Soviet Union. In that role, she met foreign leaders from around the world. She helped to develop a plan to make Germany whole again after the Berlin Wall, which had divided East and West Germany, came down. It was exciting work and gave her a key role during a momentous time in history. After serving, Rice cofounded the Center for a New Generation, a local after-school and summer program that provides academic and enrichment activities to help students succeed. The center was adopted by Boys and Girls Clubs of America and now serves students in multiple cities across the country.

> "We need to move beyond the idea that girls can be leaders and create the expectation that they should be leaders."

When George W. Bush was president, he appointed her as his national security advisor, the first woman to hold that post, and eventually secretary of state. A self-confident woman known for her hard work and sharp insights, Condoleezza Rice became a leader on the world stage. Since leaving the White House, she has continued to teach, written multiple books, cofounded an international consulting firm, and received several honorary doctorates. She has refused to let others limit what she can accomplish.

You must do the thing you think you cannot do.

ELEANOR ROOSEVELT worked tirelessly as First Lady on behalf of the American people, transforming the role into an active, political position with the power to effect change and make a difference worldwide. She became known as "the First Lady of the World."

In 1884, Eleanor was born into high society in New York City, but her childhood was not an easy one. As a young girl, she was shy and serious, characteristics that her socialite mother did not admire. Eleanor gravitated to her father, who was troubled in his own right but was a hero to his daughter. He taught her how important it was to help those less fortunate than their family. When she was six, he took her with him to serve Thanksgiving dinner to homeless boys in New York City. She was shocked by how the boys' way of life was so very different from hers, which was filled with teas, fine clothing, and pony rides. When Eleanor was eight, her mother died, and within the next two years, her young brother and her beloved father died as well. Eleanor, now an orphan, was devastated.

It wasn't until she was sent to school in England that she found a purpose. Counter to what society said about girls at the time, Eleanor's teacher Marie Souvestre taught that women had the right to live independently and speak up for themselves. Eleanor returned to New York with new confidence. She volunteered as a teacher in a settlement house, where immigrants and other people in need could find services and provisions to help them succeed. She also worked with the New York Consumers' League, helping to inspect factories for safety.

In 1905, with her uncle President Teddy Roosevelt in attendance, Eleanor married Franklin Delano Roosevelt, a man with a bright political future ahead. At first, Eleanor assumed the role of a quiet wife, but as time went on, she realized she needed to live life on her own terms, doing things that fulfilled her and made her happy.

When Franklin was elected president, the country was in the throes of the Great Depression, a time when large numbers of Americans were out of work. Eleanor traveled all over the country, acting as a liaison between the president and the people, and she also championed several programs meant to invigorate the economy. During FDR's long presidency, Eleanor wrote articles, gave speeches, and hosted her own radio shows in order to give hope to Americans during troubled times, including World War II. Perhaps the greatest contribution Eleanor offered was her unwavering support for women's rights and civil rights. Despite public pressure, she never backed down from advocating for equal treatment for all people in America.

After she left the White House, Eleanor served as the only woman in the U.S. delegation to the newly formed United Nations. In that role, she stood up for people in need around the world. The accomplishment she was most proud of was her role in the creation and adoption of the Universal Declaration of Human Rights, a document meant to ensure that people around the globe were afforded basic human rights. She continued to work toward equality for women in her role as the chair of the Presidential Commission on the Status of Women under President John F. Kennedy, the last public position she ever held.

Eleanor Roosevelt was once the most admired woman in the world because she never stopped working for the betterment of all people. Today she is still an inspiration to those fighting racism and injustice worldwide.

"We must know what we think and speak out, even at the risk of unpopularity."

MY ADVICE TO YOUNG WOMEN EVERYWHERE CONSISTS OF ONE WORD: START.

ILEANA ROS-LEHTINEN was the first Latina to serve in Congress. "I never thought, in a million years, that I would be in Congress," she has said. But serve in Congress she did, breaking stereotypes and making a difference for nearly thirty years. Her journey from an immigrant to the United States who didn't speak English to a history-making political figure who was able to work for the betterment of her country illustrates the potential and promise of America.

Ileana was born in Havana, Cuba, in 1952. When Ileana was eight years old, she and her family had to flee their country. To them, the United States represented freedom, safety, and a fresh start. Ileana has said that one of the best moments of her life was when she pledged allegiance to the flag and became a U.S. citizen. Her family lived in Miami, Florida, where she went to school and enjoyed her new, diverse community. She remembers being especially impressed with Halloween, because kids could safely walk around their neighborhoods and be given free candy.

Ileana had always wanted to be a teacher. After studying education at Florida International University, she founded a private elementary school, where she was also the principal and a teacher. Her students and their families were the ones to inspire her to run for office. She said, "My 'aha' moment was when I realized that instead of helping on a case-by-case basis, I could help many more families in South Florida by setting policy that would impact more individuals."

First, she ran for the Florida House of Representatives and won. Then she was elected to the Florida Senate. In office, she introduced the Florida Prepaid College Program, which helps students in the state afford a college education. In 1989, she ran for and won a seat in the U.S. House of Representatives. During her acceptance speech she declared in Spanish, "for our brothers listening in Cuba so they can see what a democracy is like." She didn't realize that she had made history until a television interviewer asked her how it felt to be the first Latina elected to Congress. As a U.S. representative, Ros-Lehtinen focused on women's rights around the world, pushing for girls to have better access to education and for women in Iraq to be able to hold public office. She also has said that she wants to fight to end discrimination, and she is a strong supporter of LGBTQ rights and immigration reform. As a public figure, she openly opposed tyrannical dictatorships throughout the world. She even caught the attention of Cuba's leader Fidel Castro, who called her a "ferocious she-wolf," which further motivated her to speak out.

Ros-Lehtinen made history again when she became the first woman to chair the House Committee on Foreign Affairs, where her voice was critical in crafting foreign policy around the world.

Ileana Ros-Lehtinen has won awards for her leadership, but what matters most to her has been the opportunity to serve her country and to leave her own community a better place through hard work and dedication to the issues that matter to her.

ILEANA ROS-LEHTINEN

1952–

FLORIDA STATE REPRESENTATIVE

FLORIDA STATE SENATOR

U.S. REPRESENTATIVE FROM FLORIDA

"No matter where you are from, no matter what your background is, no matter what your socioeconomic status is, every person can achieve his or her dreams."

I shall expect and feel in duty bound to make my own decisions in every case.

NELLIE TAYLOE ROSS was the first woman ever elected as governor in the United States. "Really, I dropped accidentally into politics," she told the *New York Times*. Even though her governorship rose from tragedy, it signaled a change in America.

Nellie was born in 1876 in Saint Joseph, Missouri. Her family was never financially secure. They moved to Kansas and then Nebraska, falling on hard times wherever they went. When Nellie was thirteen years old, her mother died. In response to her childhood sufferings, Nellie learned to take care of herself, to teach, and to work with other people. She managed the household and taught kindergarten and piano lessons in order to help her family.

In 1902, Nellie married William B. Ross and moved to Cheyenne, Wyoming, to start a new life. William worked as a lawyer but had his eye on politics. He served one term as a local prosecutor but lost reelection, as well as tries for further elected posts. He and Nellie agreed that campaigning took too much of a toll on their growing family, and he promised not to run again. Meanwhile, Nellie was actively involved with the Cheyenne Women's Club, where she learned public speaking and discovered her own interest in politics.

In 1922, William Ross was encouraged to run for governor and couldn't turn down the opportunity. He won, and the Rosses moved into the governor's mansion. William Ross had some big ideas for how to lead the state, and he often sought his wife's counsel. Unfortunately, two years into his term, he died. Suddenly, Nellie was faced with a difficult decision. Should she run for governor and attempt to follow through on the many ideas she and her husband had for Wyoming? Nearly everyone around her discouraged her from running: *You might hurt your reputation. Will you be able to cope emotionally if you lose?* Nellie shrugged off all the negative input and decided to run. She had a lot of bills to pay, so she needed the money, but she also had faith in her understanding of politics and wanted the chance to be governor. She threw her hat into the ring.

Wyoming had been the first state to grant women the vote. Now they had the chance to be the first state to elect a woman as governor. The voters rose to the occasion and elected Nellie Tayloe Ross with even more votes than her husband had received.

Then the real work began. There were so many things she wanted to accomplish, and Ross found that in the role of governor, she felt comfortable and powerful. She proposed ways to help farmers, enforce the prohibition of alcohol, and fund schools. Meanwhile, the nation recognized that hers was a great accomplishment, and she was invited to speak in Washington, D.C., and at the Woman's World Fair in Chicago.

Ross didn't win reelection, but she lived for 101 years, and in later life she headed the Women's Division of the Democratic National Committee and was the first woman to head the U.S. Mint, which she competently managed through a time of financial strife. Nellie Tayloe Ross stepped out of the shadows and served her country with dignity and skill.

> "The fact of my being a woman would in no way alter my obligation to the people."

Gentlemen, what is your pleasure? You are the duly elected officials of this town, I am merely your presiding officer.

SUSANNA MADORA SALTER won an election to become America's first woman mayor, in spite of the fact that her name was originally put on the ballot as a mean-spirited prank. Salter was as surprised as everyone else in her town when she won the election, but she changed history by agreeing to accept the unexpected position.

Susanna was born in 1860 in Belmont County, Ohio. When she was twelve years old, she and her family moved to a farm in Kansas. She took such high-level classes in high school that she was able to enter Kansas State Agricultural College as a second-year student, but she had to drop out before she graduated due to illness. Not too long after Susanna and her husband got married, they moved to Argonia, Kansas, where something truly remarkable happened.

Argonia was a very small town when the Salters moved there. In fact, their second child was the first baby born in the town. They named him Francis Argonia Salter. As a young mother, Susanna became involved with a local group called the Women's Christian Temperance Union (WCTU), which advocated for the prohibition of alcohol because of its harmful effects on families. The WCTU worked to support candidates who agreed with their anti-alcohol agenda, but their influence was limited because women didn't have the right to vote.

It just so happened that in 1887, women in Kansas won the right to vote locally, which immediately prompted some men who felt threatened by women's efforts to prohibit alcohol to hold a secret meeting. There they formed a plan to include Susanna Salter's name on the ballot as a candidate for mayor, thinking that the Women's Christian Temperance Union and women voters would be humiliated when Salter lost by a landslide. The whole thing was meant as a giant joke.

Knock, knock. On Election Day, a group of townspeople came to Susanna's house and informed her that she was on the ballot for mayor of Argonia. They politely asked her whether she would serve if elected.

She paused and then said yes.

This simple act, this one word, so inspired the women and some of the men of Argonia that Susanna Salter won with 60 percent of the vote. Suddenly, the joke was on the men who had maliciously put her name on the ballot. They were facing what they thought was impossible — a woman as mayor.

Mayor Salter served for a one-year term. A newspaper article stated: "She declares she will enforce the laws in their letter and spirit, without fear or favor. The women of the country will please fix their eyes on Susanna." And they did. News traveled around the country and the world that America had elected its first woman mayor. Even Susan B. Anthony, champion for women's right to vote, made a special effort to congratulate Salter. When they met, Anthony commented with surprise, "Why, you look just like any other woman."

Susanna Salter never meant to blaze any trails, but when faced with an extraordinary opportunity, she stepped up and showed the world what was possible.

> # "You were duly elected to the office of Mayor. . . . You will take due notice thereof."

I TRULY ENJOY PEOPLE AND BEING HELPFUL TO OTHERS. THAT, TO ME, IS WHAT POLITICS IS ALL ABOUT.

LOTTIE SHACKELFORD made history in 1987 when she became the first African American woman elected mayor of a major city. "A lot of people aren't aware that Little Rock is being led by a woman, a black woman mayor," she commented at the time. "It places upon one additional responsibility. It gives you a feeling of awe."

Lottie was born in Little Rock, Arkansas, in 1941. Her father was a porter and a chef for the railroad, and her mother worked in a school cafeteria and was a lab assistant. They taught Lottie and her siblings that they could be whatever they wanted. When Lottie was in high school, students in Little Rock had to go to either an all-black school or an all-white school. But that changed during Lottie's senior year.

In 1957, the National Association for the Advancement of Colored People (NAACP), in response to the Supreme Court's ruling in favor of desegregation in *Brown v. Board of Education,* attempted to register nine black students at Little Rock Central High School, an all-white school a few miles away from Lottie's school. The governor at the time was opposed to integration and sent the Arkansas National Guard to prevent the students from entering the school building. On top of facing armed men as they attempted to go to school, the brave kids were subjected to yelling, spitting, and threats by white onlookers. In response, President Dwight D. Eisenhower ordered federal troops to escort the students safely into school. Lottie wasn't one of the nine who went to Central High, but knowing that it was happening just down the street awoke in her the need to fight for equality for black Americans.

Lottie went to college with dreams of becoming a scientist. However, when her father passed away, she dropped out, and her life took a different course. She got married and had a family. Lottie joined the PTA when her kids were in school and often found herself at city hall asking for things for her local schools. Her desire to make a difference for the people of Arkansas persisted, and she felt that getting involved with local government was the best way to go. She began volunteering, stuffing envelopes and knocking on doors, in support of candidates she liked. When Lottie's kids were older, she went back to college and finished her degree, this time in business.

In 1978, she fully entered politics when she was appointed to the board of directors for Little Rock. Within ten years, she was elected as the city's first woman mayor. She used her leadership skills to support minority businesses and to speak worldwide on the importance of women in politics.

> ## "It's never about what I have done. It's what I still have yet to do."

Lottie Shackelford served as vice chair of the Democratic National Committee for twenty years and was deputy manager of President Bill Clinton's presidential campaign and part of his transition team. She has accomplished a great deal in the pursuit of creating more opportunities for women and girls and people of color. She says that even today, she has "pinch me" moments when she can hardly believe all of the amazing experiences she's had in her career. Her wish is that more African American women would get involved in politics. "We just gotta do so much more," she said. "We still have to be at the table, the congressional table, city hall table, county hall table."

LOTTIE SHACKELFORD

1941–

MAYOR OF LITTLE ROCK, ARKANSAS

My answer is short and simple— woman's proper place is everywhere.

MARGARET CHASE SMITH broke down many barriers to become the first woman to hold seats in both the House and the Senate *and* the first woman to be a contender for nomination by a major political party as a candidate for president of the United States.

Margaret was born in 1897 in Skowhegan, Maine. She was an active child who woke up early in the morning, ready to go. For most of her childhood, her family lived in her grandparents' house because they couldn't afford a home of their own.

Margaret was determined to help her family out however she could, so she marched into the local five-and-dime store and asked for a job. The man behind the counter told her he would hire her as soon as she was tall enough to reach the top shelf. Sure enough, when she was thirteen years old and a little taller, she returned to the store and got her first job.

In high school, Margaret played basketball. She loved the camaraderie among her team and felt empowered by the way they worked together to win. As high school was coming to an end, Margaret was sad to leave school and especially her team. She knew that college wasn't an option, because her parents couldn't afford it. Instead, in the years after high school, she taught, coached, and worked as a telephone operator.

Eventually, she settled in as the circulation manager of a local newspaper. She was successful in the position and became involved in civic affairs, including serving as president of the Business and Professional Women's Club of Maine. In 1930, she married businessman and town selectman Clyde Smith.

In 1936, Clyde won a seat in the House of Representatives, and the couple moved to Washington, D.C. Margaret loved living there and worked as Clyde's secretary. Then, in 1940, Clyde passed away. Before he died, he told Margaret that he wanted her to run for his seat in Congress. *Women don't belong in government,* people thought. But Margaret ran and won a special election. She served out the remainder of Clyde's term as a U.S. representative. When the term was over, she ran again. *Winning the special election to fill her husband's seat was a one-time shot,* people said. But Margaret won again. "When people keep telling you that you can't do a thing, you kind of like to try it," she said.

In fact, Margaret Chase Smith continued to win elections for the House, where she served for almost nine years, and then the Senate, where she served for twenty-four years. In office, Smith kept on challenging people's expectations for what a woman could do. She was a strong supporter of the military and the space program. She gave powerful speeches. In 1950, in a speech entitled "Declaration of Conscience," Smith boldly dared to speak out against the way American citizens were being unfairly accused of being Communists. She always wore a red rose on her lapel and advocated for the rose to be declared the official flower of the United States.

In 1964, Margaret Chase Smith ran for president, proudly putting her name in for the Republican Party's nomination. Although she didn't win the nomination, her campaign for it showed the world how far women had progressed. Throughout her career, Margaret Chase Smith made history, demonstrating determination and moral courage.

> "The right way is not always the popular and easy way. Standing for right when it is unpopular is a true test of moral character."

I do know one thing about me: I don't measure myself by others' expectations or let others define my worth.

SONIA SOTOMAYOR is the third woman and the first Latina to serve as a United States Supreme Court justice. She is an accomplished lawyer and judge who has overcome many barriers to rise to a well-deserved position on the highest court in the land. She wrote, "The challenges I have faced — among them material poverty, chronic illness, and being raised by a single mother—are not uncommon, but neither have they kept me from uncommon achievements."

Sonia was born in 1954 in the Bronx, in New York City. Her parents had moved to New York from Puerto Rico. Sonia spoke Spanish at home with her family and English at school. When she was seven years old, she learned that the reason she often felt light-headed and thirsty was that she had diabetes, a condition she would have to learn to manage for the rest of her life. Then, when she was nine, her father died unexpectedly. These were tough times for Sonia. Her mother worked hard to support the family. She bought a set of encyclopedias, the only one in the Sotomayors' whole apartment complex. These books opened the world up to Sonia. She found comfort in reading. At first she thought she wanted to become a detective after reading Nancy Drew mysteries. Then she decided she wanted to be a lawyer or maybe a judge after watching a popular television show called *Perry Mason*. It was the judge on the show, she noticed, who had the most power.

SONIA SOTOMAYOR

1954–

JUDGE, U.S. COURT OF APPEALS

SUPREME COURT JUSTICE

In high school, Sonia got a job and threw herself into her schoolwork. When her grades weren't as high as she wanted, she wasn't afraid to seek help. She asked a girl at school with high grades how she did it. The girl taught Sonia how to study. Sonia graduated from high school at the top of her class and received a full scholarship to Princeton University. At Princeton, Sonia studied hard and was active with a Puerto Rican student group. Again, she graduated at the top of her class, then went on to Yale Law School to follow her dream of being a lawyer.

She joined the district attorney's office in New York City and prosecuted many important cases. She also taught classes at New York University and Columbia Law School and volunteered in support of causes she believed in. Her career was taking off fast.

Three presidents now have asked Sotomayor to serve, and each time she stepped up. First, she was nominated by President George H. W. Bush as a judge for the Southern District of New York.

> "Understand that failure is a process in life, that only in trying can you enrich yourself and have the possibility of moving forward. The greatest obstacle in life is fear and giving up because of it."

Later, she was nominated by President Bill Clinton as a judge for the U.S. Second Circuit Court of Appeals. In 2009, Sotomayor was nominated by President Barack Obama as a Supreme Court justice. In addition to the time she spends on the court, she still does volunteer work and writes books for children and adults.

Through hard work, grit, and determination, Sonia has achieved remarkable things in her life. She has said, "You can't dream unless you know what the possibilities are." Sonia Sotomayor is a shining example of what is possible.

No country ever has had or ever will have peace until every citizen has a voice in the government.

ELIZABETH CADY STANTON grew up in a world where women were considered second-class citizens, a fact of life she was determined to change. She was perhaps the most prominent leader in the women's fight for equal rights and the first woman to run for Congress.

Elizabeth was born in 1815 in Johnstown, New York. From a young age, she was keyed in to the inequities between boys and girls, men and women. After her baby sister was born, Elizabeth overheard her parents lament that the baby wasn't a boy.

And when her older brother died, her grief-stricken father told Elizabeth directly how much he wished that she had been a boy.

As a bright and capable girl, Elizabeth couldn't understand why everyone seemed to prefer boys, and from that point on, she was determined to show that girls could do all the things that boys could do. She practiced debate and Greek until she could beat the boys in competitions. She conquered daring feats on horseback that only boys were supposed to try. Sadly, her efforts weren't admired as much as she hoped. Her family and society just repeated over and over that girls were meant to stay in the home, not win at things, not participate in public life. But Elizabeth didn't settle for that then, nor did she for the rest of her life. She was convinced that the whole world was wrong, so she set out to challenge the conventions of her day.

When her father said she had to quit school at age fifteen, she argued that it was unfair since her brother had continued his education past that age and she was at least as intelligent as he was. Her father relented. When Elizabeth and Henry Stanton, a dedicated abolitionist, were married, she refused to say that she would "obey" him, as was required in the standard wedding vows. And when the leadership of the country supported slavery, Elizabeth and other fervent abolitionists took a stand against it. But it was women's rights that she fought for the hardest.

In 1848, she and a handful of other women decided to hold the first women's rights convention, in Seneca Falls, New York. In preparation, they wrote what they called a Declaration of Sentiments, which stated, "We hold these truths to be self-evident: that all men and women are created equal," and declared that women deserved the right to vote. After they announced the meeting, they waited, unsure if anyone would show up. To their surprise and delight, more than one hundred people poured in for the convention, a moment that marked the beginning of the women's movement in the United States.

In 1854, Elizabeth bravely spoke to the New York legislature about women's rights, and although her speech didn't lead to any immediate change, it stuck in the minds of the congressmen. Moreover, fifty thousand copies of the speech were circulated nationally. In 1866, she ran for Congress, the first woman ever to do so. She did it just to show that women could, even though she received only twenty-four votes.

Elizabeth Cady Stanton's conviction that women are capable, intelligent, and worthy of equal rights was considered radical during her lifetime, but today her ideas are commonly held. She was way ahead of her time, and sadly she never did get to vote. But her voice and her determination changed the world.

ELIZABETH CADY STANTON

1815–1902

SUFFRAGIST LEADER

ACTIVIST

FIRST WOMAN CANDIDATE FOR U.S. HOUSE OF REPRESENTATIVES

"The right is ours, have it we must — use it we will. The pens, the tongues, the fortunes, the indomitable wills of many women are already pledged to secure this right."

And so, lifting as we climb, onward and upward we go.

MARY CHURCH TERRELL was a writer, a speaker, a teacher, an activist, and one of the first African American women appointed to the school board of a major city. She became political because she wanted to see change in the country, and she skillfully used everything she had in her quest for social justice.

Mary was born in 1863 in Memphis, Tennessee. Her parents were both formerly enslaved people who, once emancipated, established themselves as successful business owners in their community. Her mother owned a popular hair salon, and her father was a real-estate investor. Mary was sent away to an integrated school in Ohio at six years old. She loved school and continued all the way through until she graduated from Oberlin College, one of the first colleges in the United States to admit African Americans.

She returned home full of ambition and ideas. "All during my college course I had dreamed of the day when I could promote the welfare of my race," she said. Her father, however, wanted her to lead the life of a lady. She did so for a while, but Mary had opinions, ideas, and talents, and she wanted to share them. So she packed her bags and worked as a teacher, first in Ohio, then in Washington, D.C. She went back to Oberlin and earned her master's degree in education, then left for Europe to learn more about the world.

When she returned to the United States, she resumed teaching and married Robert Terrell. At the time, she struggled with depression, partly because a good friend of hers was lynched   taken away by an angry mob and hanged from a tree to die. She was witness to the terrifying and unjust treatment of African Americans, and she felt more strongly than ever that she had to do something.

As the first black woman to ever serve on the board of education in Washington, D.C., Mary Church Terrell championed equal education for the city's African American students. She gave voice to children who had never been represented before.

In addition, at that time in history, it was risky for a woman to publicly declare her support for women's suffrage, but it was a risk Mary was willing to take. She was brave and stood up for what she believed in, sometimes literally. Once, at a crowded suffragist meeting, when the presiding officer asked those who believed in women's right to vote to stand up, Terrell looked around, and even though no one else stood at first, she courageously rose to her feet.

Terrell also understood the power in getting women to work together. She started small, banding together with other African American women in D.C., and eventually helped link small groups all over the country to create the National Association of Colored Women, of which she served as the first president.

Powered by her unwavering belief in civil rights, Mary Church Terrell lived by her own words: "I will take an active interest in the welfare of my country, using my influence toward the enactment of laws for the protection of the unfortunate and weak and for the repeal of those depriving human beings of their privileges and rights." She went all over the world spreading her message about racial injustice by giving speeches and writing both books and hundreds of articles for magazines and newspapers. She campaigned for political candidates she believed in. She educated African Americans about their right to vote. She protested. She never relented.

"We knock at the bar of justice, asking an equal chance."

KEEP JUST A LITTLE SPACE IN YOUR HEART FOR THE IMPROBABLE. I PROMISE YOU WON'T REGRET IT.

ELIZABETH WARREN is the senior senator from Massachusetts. She is known as an expert in matters of economics and as a woman who fights for what she believes in.

Elizabeth was born in 1949 in Oklahoma City, Oklahoma. When she was in second grade, she told a beloved teacher that she also wanted to be a teacher when she grew up. Her teacher encouraged her, but Elizabeth's mother didn't support this dream. She believed that a woman should not work outside the home. Things changed when Elizabeth's father had a heart attack and was demoted at his job. Her mother had to work so their family could pay the bills. Elizabeth pitched in by waiting tables at her aunt's restaurant.

In high school, Elizabeth was a star debater. She didn't do sports or play an instrument, but she was great at making strong arguments to support her viewpoints. Even though her mother did not want her to go to college, Elizabeth applied to schools and received a full scholarship to George Washington University, leaving her mother little reason to say no.

Elizabeth left college to get married at the young age of nineteen. She and her husband moved to Houston, Texas, where she completed her degree. She was the first person in her family to graduate from college, and she was finally able to teach, as she had always wanted. When her two children were small, she earned her law degree. Eventually she found an opportunity to teach law students, a job that satisfied many of her professional and family needs at the time.

While teaching, Warren became interested in learning about economic factors that affect middle-class families in America. She studied these issues and moved around the country with her second husband before settling into a job as a law professor at Harvard University. As a professor, Warren started talking about how everyday Americans were being hurt financially by banks, payday lenders, and other financial companies. She proposed the need for an agency that would protect consumers by regulating such companies. As a result, the Consumer Financial Protection Bureau was created. In 2010, President Barack Obama named Warren as an assistant to the president and a special advisor to the treasury secretary on the brand-new agency.

Motivated to support working and middle-class families, Elizabeth ran for Senate in 2012 and won. During a debate on the Senate floor, Warren attempted to read aloud a letter written by Coretta Scott King to show her disapproval of a presidential nomination. She was told to be silent, but she kept talking. In response, Senate Majority Leader Mitch McConnell infamously said, "She was warned. She was given an explanation. Nevertheless, she persisted." The phrase "Nevertheless, she persisted" has since become a battle cry for women's rights and is associated with Elizabeth Warren's career.

In February 2019, Warren officially declared her candidacy for president.

> ## "Women vote, organize marches, knock on doors, make phone calls, run for office — and win."

The people must know before they can act, and there is no educator to compare with the press.

IDA B. WELLS-BARNETT was an intrepid journalist who believed in the power of the pen to expose truth and bring about justice. She used research, writing, and organizing to effect political change in America.

Ida was born in 1862, during the Civil War, in Holly Springs, Mississippi. She and her family lived as enslaved people until the conflict ended and the U.S. Constitution was amended to end slavery. Ida's parents shared stories of their lives in slavery, and Ida listened. Once she learned to read, she read the newspaper to her father, a politically minded carpenter who voted for Republican candidates in homage to the Republican president Abraham Lincoln and worked for equality for African Americans throughout his life.

One day, in Memphis, Ida bought a first-class train ticket and took her seat in the ladies' car. When told to move, she refused. She braced her feet against the seat in front of her and tried her hardest to stay put. She held on until eventually three men forced her out. This incident changed Ida forever. She became a journalist and a partner in a newspaper, writing about injustice.

When three of Ida's friends were lynched, Ida wrote powerful articles in the newspaper about their brutal murders. Some people became enraged at her candor and burned down her newspaper office, but Ida continued to write. She became known as the "Princess of the Press," and her daring words had a great effect. At one point, they sparked a boycott of the streetcars in Memphis. And when she called for African Americans to leave Memphis and head west for more freedom, thousands of people answered the call.

After she had a family, Ida Wells-Barnett found a way to balance motherhood with her activism. Just about any time she learned of injustice, she went to work. She linked up with other influential people, such as Frederick Douglass and Susan B. Anthony. She started clubs for people who wanted to make a difference. She gave speeches and she wrote and wrote and wrote—her articles were circulated around the world. Wells-Barnett took her concerns all the way to the White House, where she talked with President William McKinley about the dire need to stop lynching in America.

Wells-Barnett believed there was power in numbers. She fought for women's voting rights, marching alongside other suffragists in Washington, D.C., and started the Alpha Suffrage Club in 1913. She joined clubs of women working together and was involved in founding the National Association for the Advancement of Colored People (NAACP), still one of the most powerful groups fighting for racial equality today. Later in life, Wells-Barnett ran for a seat in the Illinois State Senate. Even though she didn't win, her run paved the way for other black women to seek office.

Ida B. Wells-Barnett spoke up, stood strong, and bravely fought for what she believed in by investigating and writing articles that exposed the truth about racist practices in her country. Her grit and determination are shining examples of how one person can be a force for good in this world.

IDA B. WELLS-BARNETT

1862–1931

JOURNALIST

ACTIVIST

STATE SENATORIAL CANDIDATE

> ## "The way to right wrongs is to turn the light of truth upon them."

All the threads in the tangled fabric of the world's history laid in my hands for a few minutes.

EDITH WILSON was called "the secret president." America has yet to elect a woman in her own right for the office, but did you know that for a year and a half, First Lady Edith Wilson in effect acted as president of the United States when her husband, Woodrow Wilson, was too ill to lead?

Edith was born in 1872 in Wytheville, Virginia. Her family was financially devastated after the Civil War and moved into a small brick house, where Edith took care of her ailing grandmother. There wasn't enough money to send Edith to school, so her grandmother taught her to read and write at home. At fifteen years old, Edith had a chance to go away to school to study music. She was miserable there, hungry, cold, and homesick, so she tried another school. Unfortunately, money was so tight that her father made the decision to pull Edith from her new school. All told, she had only two years of formal education.

When she turned eighteen, Edith met Norman Galt in Washington, D.C., and the two married several years later. After eleven years of marriage, Norman died, and Edith was left with his jewelry business. Back then, it was uncommon for a woman to run a business, but that's what Edith decided to do. Under her leadership, the business did so well that she was able to buy a car. A woman driving her own car was a rare sight to behold in those days, but Edith drove with pride.

In March 1915, Edith was invited to the White House by President Woodrow Wilson's cousin. Wilson, grief stricken since his wife's death, saw something special in Edith from the moment they met. At the end of that year, the two were married. Suddenly, while World War I was underway and heating up in Europe, Edith was America's First Lady. President Wilson and Edith shared a unique connection. He considered her a partner in the presidency. Edith played an active role in helping with her husband's presidential and wartime duties: she attended meetings and even decoded encrypted military messages. She also volunteered with the Red Cross and raised war funds by auctioning off wool from sheep that grazed on the White House lawn. Wilson confided in her and sought her opinion on matters of state.

In 1919, President Wilson had a stroke; he had great difficulty speaking and was partially paralyzed. He could no longer function as president, but instead of alarming the nation with the news of his condition, Edith took on the role of president herself. Just as she had with the jewelry business after her first husband died, Edith stepped up — this time, to run the country. She acted as an intermediary between the president and the rest of the world, deciding what was important enough to bring to his attention. But more than that, she monitored

"A completely gifted woman." — Woodrow Wilson

foreign policy and was involved in appointing members to the cabinet. From 1919 until the end of President Wilson's term in 1921, the power of the presidency flowed through Edith Wilson. During a time of crisis, she managed to keep the country running smoothly enough that most people had no idea the president was incapacitated.

No, she didn't win an election. Nor did she receive recognition for what she did. But history shows that Edith Wilson, with a knack for politics and leadership, was the first woman to act as president of the United States.

Women have every right. All they need to do is exercise them.

VICTORIA WOODHULL was the first woman to run for president of the United States. She was a brave advocate for women's rights who bucked the traditions of her day to stand up for what she believed was fair for women and to demonstrate that women were capable of taking charge of their own lives.

Victoria was born in 1838 in Homer, Ohio. She had a difficult childhood, but she always believed she was a leader destined for great things. She lived with her parents and nine brothers and sisters in a small cabin, and her family often did not have enough money for food. While her siblings would knock on doors and beg their neighbors for scraps, Victoria knocked on doors and asked for work so she could make her own money. From a young age, she showed a talent for public speaking and would preach Bible stories to a captivated audience. People liked to listen to what she had to say.

Victoria always worked to support herself and her family. She believed that the ability to earn money of her own was the key to a woman's independence. After Victoria escaped an unhappy marriage, she and her sister Tennessee Claflin traveled around, working as fortune-tellers and healers. They ended up in New York, a bustling city with horse-drawn carriages and streets lit by gas lamps. Even though Victoria had hardly any formal education, she had street smarts and made some wise investments in the stock market, which earned her a lot of money. Cornelius Vanderbilt, one of the richest men in the world, was one of the sisters' fortune-telling clients. He was so impressed with Victoria's stock market predictions that he lent the sisters money to open up their own business, making Victoria and Tennessee the first women stockbrokers in the history of the United States. They used the money they made to start a weekly newspaper, in which they published their views about how women should be treated equally to men.

Even Susan B. Anthony and Elizabeth Cady Stanton, two of the leaders of the American women's suffrage movement, noticed Victoria Woodhull's success. Woodhull took up the cause and fought passionately for women's right to vote. She argued in front of the U.S. House Judiciary Committee that women *already had* the right to vote according to the Fourteenth and Fifteenth Amendments to the Constitution. On Election Day 1871, she led a group of women to the polls and attempted to cast a ballot. A crowd of men came forward. Laughing, they refused to allow her to approach the ballot box. She was discouraged at first but later gave a rousing speech about the experience.

Even though women weren't allowed to vote, there was no law that said they couldn't run for political office. Woodhull went straight to the top and declared her candidacy for president of the United States under the Equal Rights Party. She knew she'd be criticized, but now she had a platform from which to speak about what she believed in: that women deserved the same rights as men in the United States to vote, to work, and to be free. Victoria Woodhull didn't win — in fact on Election Day she was in jail for something controversial she had published in her newspaper — but she used her voice and fought with great bravery to make a difference for women in the United States.

VICTORIA WOODHULL

1838–1927

SUFFRAGIST

NEWSPAPER EDITOR

PRESIDENTIAL CANDIDATE

"What is there left women to do but to become the mothers of the future government."

HOW TO STAND UP, SPEAK OUT, AND MAKE A DIFFERENCE: A TAKE-ACTION GUIDE

The women in this book have accomplished some pretty amazing things. They are brave and brilliant. They are persistent and tough. They are loud. They are quiet. They are strong.

They are no different from you.

No two leaders in this book are alike. Some are from big cities, others from small towns. Some were born into families with a lot of money; others were not. They come from different cultural, religious, and political backgrounds.

When you read a biography, you might decide that the person you're learning about was extra special or that they must have known things you don't know. But we are here to tell you that if you want to make a difference, you've already got what it takes. All the women in this book started with the simple desire to make a difference. They took an interest in the world. They had ideas for how to change their country and how to improve life for their fellow citizens.

Have you ever felt like you had something important to say?

Do you have an idea for how to make something better in your community?

Is there an aspect of the world that you'd like to change?

Have you ever wanted to make a difference but weren't sure how?

Next to each biography in this book, you'll find highlighted some of the tactics the woman used to make change. There isn't one key to becoming a leader. No single secret to success. Time and time again, it's the little steps that people take that add up to make a big difference. As Justice Ruth Bader Ginsburg said, "Real change, enduring change, happens one step at a time." So don't be afraid to take that first step.

Here are some tips to help you stand up, speak out, and make a difference.

START WITH YOUR COMMUNITY

Your community is the place you know best — your neighborhood, your school, your town or city, maybe your state. There are issues all over the world that need addressing, and it can feel overwhelming. But if you start small, a change you make close to home can spread and have an effect on a larger scale, like a ripple in a pond.

You know what you love about your community, and you may have ideas for how things can be improved. You also know the people in your community and can identify who can help: someone like a parent, a teacher, a principal, a coach, or a police officer.

Local issues that kids are speaking up about in their communities include school safety, dress codes, anti-bullying, and green practices such as recycling.

Look around. What matters to you?

STAY INFORMED

Learn all you can about the issues that are important to you. Read the newspaper. Read books. Watch the news. Get online and search. Seek out people who know a lot and ask them to share what they know. Listen.

The more informed you are, the better you will be at making change. Don't worry — you don't have to be an expert or know every single detail about what's going on. But facts do matter.

It's also a good idea to look at multiple sides of an issue so you can understand all the different perspectives surrounding your topic and take into consideration how other people feel.

Have you ever heard the phrase "Knowledge is power"? It's a popular saying because it's true. The more you know, the more effective a leader you will be.

VOLUNTEER; JOIN AN EXISTING GROUP

While you're learning everything you can about an issue, you might find out that there's already a group of people who are working on the same thing. Join forces! You won't have to start from scratch. Chances are, if there is an existing group you can get involved with, they've done a lot of the groundwork. See how you can help. They might need someone to make phone calls or write postcards. They might hold a rally that you can attend. You and your talents might be just what they need to succeed. And if there's not an existing group — you can start one!

ORGANIZE

Imagine one person standing up for something important. Now imagine two, three, ten, one hundred.

It can be a lot easier to make change when more than one person is working on a problem. Reach out to people you know who might be interested in helping. Set up an after-school meeting to make a plan. Shirley Chisholm used to get people together just to inform them about the issues. As a group, you can make posters, write post-cards, and organize events.

Be inclusive. The more diverse your group is, the more talents you'll have to work with. If you're inclusive, people will want to join you to pursue a common goal.

SPREAD THE WORD

If you have an idea, let people know. Share it. Hang posters. Hand out flyers. If you are over thirteen, perhaps you'll decide to use social media in responsible and positive ways. Make phone calls. Talk about it.

Communicating your ideas is an important step in making change.

Make sure the tone you use is positive and engaging so that more people will listen and respond.

BRING YOUR OWN TALENTS

You are unique and have your own set of talents that you can employ to help make a difference in the world. No one needs to be perfect at everything! Maybe you are great at debating or arguing your side. Maybe you're a strong writer who can write letters or emails or postcards. Maybe you're an artist who can make posters to spread the word. Some people are gifted at including people and helping them get involved. Others are good at research. What's your special talent?

STAY POSITIVE

Try not to get discouraged. There is rarely a straight path that leads to success and change. Most of the women in this book climbed past giant obstacles throughout their lives. Almost all of them failed at some point. But they got back up, learned from the experience, and tried again.

One of the great things about America is that there is the promise, the potential, for anyone to emerge as a leader and to make this world a better place. Your name doesn't have to be Sandra Day O'Connor, Shirley Chisholm, or Hillary Rodham Clinton for you to be a strong leader, but you can begin by learning about the things other leaders did on their path to leadership. The United States still hasn't elected a woman as president. You could be the first — or maybe even the fifth. The women before our time have helped lead the way for us today, and we must look ahead to the future of our country.

You are that future.

STACEY ABRAMS

1973–

Georgia state representative, minority leader of the Georgia House of Representatives, gubernatorial candidate

JULIA C. ADDINGTON

1829–1875

Superintendent of schools for Mitchell County, Iowa

CORA REYNOLDS ANDERSON

1882–1950

Michigan state representative

SILA MARÍA CALDERÓN

1942–

Secretary of state of Puerto Rico, mayor of San Juan, governor of Puerto Rico

ELAINE CHAO

1953–

U.S. secretary of labor, U.S. secretary of transportation

SUSAN COLLINS

1952–

U.S. senator from Maine

CATHERINE CORTEZ MASTO

1964–

Attorney general of Nevada, U.S. senator from Nevada

CLARA CRESSINGHAM

1863–1906

Colorado state representative

SHARICE DAVIDS

1980–

U.S. representative from Kansas

JONI ERNST

1970–

Iowa state senator, U.S. senator from Iowa

TULSI GABBARD

1981–

Hawaii state representative, U.S. representative from Hawaii, presidential candidate

FEDELINA LUCERO GALLEGOS

Served 1931–1932

New Mexico state representative

GABRIELLE GIFFORDS

1970–

Arizona state representative, Arizona state senator, U.S. representative from Arizona

KIRSTEN GILLIBRAND

1966–

U.S. representative from New York, U.S. senator from New York, presidential candidate

DEB HAALAND

1960–

U.S. representative from New Mexico

GINA HASPEL

1956–

Director of the U.S. Central Intelligence Agency

PRAMILA JAYAPAL

1965–

Washington state senator, U.S. representative from Washington

AMY KLOBUCHAR

1960–

U.S. senator from Minnesota, presidential candidate

LORI LIGHTFOOT

1962–

Mayor of Chicago

MIA LOVE

1975–

Mayor of Saratoga Springs, Utah; U.S. representative from Utah

BARBARA MIKULSKI

1936–

U.S. representative from Maryland, U.S. senator from Maryland

LISA MURKOWSKI

1957–

Alaska state representative, U.S. senator from Alaska

JANET NAPOLITANO

1957–

U.S. attorney for the district of Arizona, attorney general of Arizona, governor of Arizona, U.S. secretary of homeland security

ANTONIA NOVELLO

1944–

U.S. surgeon general

ILHAN OMAR

1982–

Minnesota state representative, U.S. representative from Minnesota

DANICA ROEM

1984–

Member of the Virginia House of Delegates

PORFIRRIA HIDALGO SAIZ

Served 1931–1932

New Mexico state representative

RASHIDA TLAIB

1976–

Michigan state representative, U.S. representative from Michigan

CHRISTINE TODD WHITMAN

1946–

Governor of New Jersey, administrator of the U.S. Environmental Protection Agency

MARIANNE WILLIAMSON

1952–

Presidential candidate

p. iv: "You can't dream . . . possibilities are": quoted in Tom McGhee, "Justice Sotomayor: New Justice Center a 'Magnificent Tribute,'" *Denver Post,* May 2, 2013, https://www.denverpost .com/2013/05/02/justice-sotomayor-new-justice-center-a-magnificent-tribute/.

Foreword
p. ix: "If they don't . . . folding chair": quoted in Vanessa Williams, "'Unbought and Unbossed': Shirley Chisholm's Feminist Mantra Is Still Relevant 50 Years Later," *Washington Post,* January 26, 2018, https://www.washingtonpost.com/news/post-nation/wp/2018/01/26/unbought -and-unbossed-shirley-chisholms-feminist-mantra-is-as-relevant-today-as-it-was-50-years -ago/?utm_term=.e6d691dd4998.

Introduction
p. 2: "My pen runs riot": Abigail Adams to John Adams, May 12, 1776, Adams Family Papers: An Electronic Archive, Massachusetts Historical Society, http://www.masshist.org/digitaladams /archive/.

p. 2: "This woman's place . . . Representatives!": Yanker Poster Collection, Library of Congress Prints and Photographs Division, 1971, https://www.loc.gov/item/2016648584/.

Bella Abzug
p. 6: "This woman's place . . . Representatives!": Yanker Poster Collection, Library of Congress Prints and Photographs Division, 1971, https://www.loc.gov/item/2016648584/.

p. 7: "We take no females": quoted in Alan H. Levy, *The Political Life of Bella Abzug, 1920–1976: Political Passions, Women's Rights, and Congressional Battles* (New York: Lexington Books, 2013), 18.

p. 7: "Women are not wedded . . . didn't let us": Bella Abzug, "Plenary Speech, Fourth World Conference on Women" (speech, Beijing, China, September 12, 1995), Iowa State University Archives of Women's Political Communication, https://awpc.cattcenter.iastate.edu/2017/03 /21/plenary-speech-fourth-world-conference-on-women-sept-12-1995/.

p. 7: "There are those . . . serious woman": Bella S. Abzug, *Bella!: Ms. Abzug Goes to Washington* (New York: Saturday Review Press, 1972), 3.

Abigail Adams
p. 8: "I desire you . . . your ancestors": Abigail Adams to John Adams, March 31–April 5, 1776, Adams Family Papers: An Electronic Archive, Massachusetts Historical Society, http://www .masshist.org/digitaladams/archive/.

p. 9: "You are a Politician . . . the Tory Ladies": John Adams to Abigail Adams, May 12, 1776, Adams Family Papers: An Electronic Archive, Massachusetts Historical Society, http://www .masshist.org/digitaladams/archive/.

p. 9: "Do not put such . . . voice, or Representation": Abigail Adams to John Adams, March

31–April 5, 1776, Adams Family Papers: An Electronic Archive, Massachusetts Historical Society, http://www.masshist.org/digitaladams/archive/.

p. 9: "I will never . . . point of light": Abigail Adams to Elizabeth Smith Shaw Peabody, July 19, 1799, National Archives, Founders Online, https://founders.archives.gov/documents /Adams/99-03-02-0428.

Madeleine Albright
p. 10: "It took me . . . to be silent": Madeleine Albright, "Madeleine Albright: An Exclusive Interview," interview by Marianne Schnall, *Huffington Post,* June 15, 2010, https://www .huffpost.com/entry/madeleine-albright-an-exc_n_604418.

p. 10: "I never expected to be who I am": ibid.

p. 11: "Real leadership . . . to doing": Madeleine Albright, "Commencement Address at Chapel Hill at the University of North Carolina" (speech, Chapel Hill, NC, May 13, 2007), University of North Carolina Alumni Association website, audio, 7:14, https://alumni.unc.edu/realaudio/grad2007 /007.mp3.

p. 11: "The reason I . . . economically empowered": Madeleine Albright, "Madeleine Albright: An Exclusive Interview."

Tammy Baldwin
p. 12: "Don't listen to . . . Just do it": Tammy Baldwin, "Tammy Baldwin, United States Senator, Wisconsin," *Makers,* PBS, video, 4:44, https://www.makers.com/profiles /591f26af4d21a801db72e82c/554594aee4b042cdf60f3728.

p. 12: "I thought I . . . my own risk": Tammy Baldwin, "Commencement Address at Smith College" (speech, Northampton, MA, May 17, 2009), Iowa State University Archives of Women's Political Communication, https://awpc.cattcenter.iastate.edu/2017/03/21/commencement-address-at -smith-college-may-17-2009/.

p. 13: "Have faith in . . . faith in others": ibid.

Mary McLeod Bethune
p. 14: "I am a believer . . . their possibilities": quoted in Amy Robin Jones, *Mary McLeod Bethune* (Mankato, MN: Child's World, 2009), 17.

p. 15: "Our children . . . a better world": Mary McLeod Bethune, "My Last Will and Testament," Bethune-Cookman University, https://www.cookman.edu/about_bcu/history/lastwill _testament.html.

p. 15: "I leave you love . . . racial dignity": ibid.

Hattie Wyatt Caraway
p. 16: "The die is cast . . . to tradition": Hattie Wyatt Caraway, *Silent Hattie Speaks: The Personal Journal of Senator Hattie Caraway,* ed. Diane D. Kincaid (Westport, CT: Greenwood, 1979), 126.

p. 17: "Although she made . . . general election": Nancy Hendricks, *Senator Hattie Caraway: An Arkansas Legacy* (Charleston, SC: History Press, 2013), 28.

p. 17: "I really want . . . for office": Hattie Wyatt Caraway, *Silent Hattie Speaks,* 121.

p. 17: "The time has . . . for the job": quoted in "Caraway, Hattie Wyatt," United States House of Representatives: History, Art & Archives, https://history.house.gov/People/Listing/C/CARAWAY,-Hattie-Wyatt-(C000138)/.

Soledad Chávez Chacón

p. 18: "The affairs of . . . administration": quoted in Doris Weatherford, *Women in American Politics: History and Milestones* (Los Angeles: Sage, 2012), 73.

p. 19: "It is my earnest . . . his policy": quoted in Deborah Baker, "'Lala' Was New Mexico's First Female Governor," *Albuquerque Journal,* October 24, 2010, https://www.abqjournal.com/elex/2010generalelection/2010governorrace/2403252010governorrace10-24-10.htm.

Shirley Chisholm

p. 20: "If they don't . . . folding chair": quoted in Vanessa Williams, "'Unbought and Unbossed': Shirley Chisholm's Feminist Mantra Is Still Relevant 50 Years Later," *Washington Post,* January 26, 2018, https://www.washingtonpost.com/news/post-nation/wp/2018/01/26/unbought-and-unbossed-shirley-chisholms-feminist-mantra-is-as-relevant-today-as-it-was-50-years-ago/?utm_term=.e6d691dd4998.

p. 20: "Fighting . . . Unbossed": Shirley Chisholm, *Unbought and Unbossed* (Boston: Houghton Mifflin, 1970), 69.

p. 21: "You don't make . . . implementing ideas": quoted in Harold Jackson, "Shirley Chisholm: The First Black Woman Elected to Congress, She Was an Outspoken Advocate Against Discrimination," *The Guardian,* January 3, 2005, https://www.theguardian.com/news/2005/jan/04/guardianobituaries.haroldjackson.

p. 21: "Tremendous amounts . . . a skirt": Shirley Chisholm, *Unbought and Unbossed,* 92.

p. 21: "I want history . . . in America": Shirley Chisholm, "Excerpts from the National Visionary Leadership Project," interview by Camille O. Cosby, May 7, 2002, Iowa State University Archives of Women's Political Communication, https://awpc.cattcenter.iastate.edu/2017/03/09/excerpts-from-the-national-visionary-leadership-project-may-7-2002/.

Hillary Rodham Clinton

p. 22: "To every little . . . even president": Hillary Rodham Clinton (@Hillary Clinton), Twitter, June 7, 2016, 6:08 p.m., https://twitter.com/HillaryClinton/status/740349871073398785.

p. 23: "Human rights . . . human rights": Hillary Rodham Clinton, "Women's Rights Are Human Rights" (speech, Beijing, China, October 5, 1995), Iowa State University Archives of Women's Political Communication, https://awpc.cattcenter.iastate.edu/2017/03/21/womens-rights-are-human-rights-oct-5-1995/.

p. 23: "I know we still . . . someone will": Hillary Rodham Clinton, "Presidential Concession Speech" (speech, New York, NY, November 9, 2016), Iowa State University Archives of Women's Political Communication, https://awpc.cattcenter.iastate.edu/2017/03/21/presidential-concession-speech-nov-9-2016/.

Elizabeth Dole

p. 24: "Freedom empowers . . . glass ceilings": Elizabeth Dole, "Remarks at the 2000 Republican National Convention," (speech, Philadelphia, PA, August 2, 2000), Iowa State University Archives of Women's Political Communication, https://awpc.cattcenter.iastate.edu/2017/03/09/remarks-at-the-2000-rnc-aug-2-2000/.

p. 24: "Women share . . . role models": quoted in Kathy Nellis, *CNN Newsroom,* August 24, 2001, http://www.cnn.com/TRANSCRIPTS/0108/24/nr.00.html.

p. 25: "When you're . . . for people?": quoted in Susan Chira, "After the Flood with: Elizabeth Hanford Dole; Power Player, Playing Cautiously," *New York Times,* October 20, 1993, https://www.nytimes.com/1993/10/20/garden/after-the-flood-with-elizabeth-hanford-dole-power-player-playing-cautiously.html.

Tammy Duckworth

p. 26: "I have to . . . want to be": quoted in Kayla Webley Adler, "We Have More Female Senators Than Ever Before — Here Are the Four New Ones to Watch," *Marie Claire,* February 13, 2017, https://www.marieclaire.com/culture/news/a25342/new-female-us-senators/.

p. 26: "The lessons . . . who I am": Tammy Duckworth, "Take Sexual Assault Prosecutions out of Military Chain of Command," *Chicago Tribune,* June 7, 2013, https://www.chicagotribune.com/opinion/ct-xpm-2013-06-07-ct-perspec-0607-assault-20130607-story.html.

p. 27: "These legs . . . don't buckle": quoted in Megan Carpentier, "Tammy Duckworth Shows Her Strength in Senate Fight: 'These Legs Don't Buckle,'" *The Guardian,* August 25, 2016, https://www.theguardian.com/us-news/2016/aug/25/tammy-duckworth-senate-race-illinois-profile.

p. 27: "It's important . . . we can fix": quoted in Kayla Webley Adler, "We Have More Female Senators."

Crystal Bird Fauset

p. 28: "No people . . . for themselves": "Crystal Bird Fauset Quits Democrats; Supports Dewey," *Pittsburgh Courier,* September 16, 1944, 1, Newspapers.com.

p. 29: "to lift the curtain of misunderstanding": quoted in "Lifting the Curtain: Crystal Bird Fauset," American Friends Service Committee website, March 30, 2010, https://www.afsc.org/story/lifting-curtain-crystal-bird-fauset.

p. 29: "We should not want . . . real democracy": *Women's Centennial Congress, New York, 1940,* 56, Mary Church Terrell Papers, Subject File 1884–1962, Library of Congress, https://www.loc.gov/item/mss425490339/.

Dianne Feinstein

p. 30: "Doors have opened . . . more to do": Dianne Feinstein, "The Power of Women" (speech, Century City, CA, March 22, 2006), Iowa State University Archives of Women's Political Communication, https://awpc.cattcenter.iastate.edu/2017/03/21/power-of-women-march-22-2006/.

p. 31: "Heroism . . . sexual orientation": 139 Cong. Rec. 2179 (February 4, 1993) (statement of Senator Dianne Feinstein).

Geraldine Ferraro

p. 32: "Some leaders are born women": Geraldine A. Ferraro, "The Future of Women in Politics" (speech, New York, NY, February 20, 1991), Iowa State University Archives of Women's Political

Communication, https://awpc.cattcenter.iastate.edu/2017/03/09/the-future-of-women-in
-politics-feb-20-1991/.

p. 33: "We've chosen . . . turn us around": Geraldine A. Ferraro, *Ferraro: My Story* (Evanston, IL:
Northwestern University Press, 2004), 268.

p. 33: "I stand before . . . all of us": Geraldine A. Ferraro, "Inspiration from the Land Where
Dreams Come True" (speech, San Francisco, CA, July 19, 1984), Iowa State University Archives of
Women's Political Communication, https://awpc.cattcenter.iastate.edu/2017/03/21/inspiration
-from-the-land-where-dreams-come-true-july-19-1984/.

Betty Ford
p. 34: "Being ladylike . . . silence": Betty Ford, "Remarks to the International Women's Year
Conference," (speech, Cleveland, OH, October 25, 1975), Gerald R. Ford Presidential Library and
Museum, https://www.fordlibrarymuseum.gov/library/bbfspeeches/751025.asp.

p. 35: "The long road . . . everyday life": ibid.

Ruth Bader Ginsburg
p. 36: "So often in life . . . good fortune": Ruth Bader Ginsburg, "Ruth Bader Ginsburg: Rejected
by the Firm," *Makers,* PBS, June 12, 2012, video, 1:16, https://www.youtube.com/watch?v=
ldFUmU-OZ1U.

p. 36: "My mother . . . independent": quoted in Nina Totenberg, "Justice Ruth Bader Ginsburg's
Life Immortalized in Song," *Morning Edition,* NPR, July 18, 2018, https://www.npr.org/2018/07
/18/623893240/justice-ruth-bader-ginsburgs-life-immortalized-in-song.

p. 37: "People ask me . . . there are nine": Ruth Bader Ginsburg, "Dean's Lecture to the
Graduating Class," interview by William M. Treanor, Georgetown University Law Center, CSPAN,
February 4, 2015, video, 46:08, https://www.c-span.org/video/?324177-1/discussion-supreme
-court-justice-ruth-bader-ginsburg.

p. 37: "I try to teach . . . men or women": Ruth Bader Ginsburg, "Exclusive Justice Ruth Bader
Ginsburg Interview: Full Transcript," interview by Irin Carmon, *The Rachel Maddow Show,*
MSNBC, February 16, 2015, http://www.msnbc.com/msnbc/exclusive-justice-ruth-bader
-ginsburg-interview-full-transcript.

Ella T. Grasso
p. 38: "The governorship . . . people's job": quoted in Susan Bysiewicz, *Ella: A Biography of
Governor Ella Grasso* (Old Saybrook, CT: Peregrine, 1984), 73.

p. 38: "I realized . . . decision-making process": quoted in Shirley Washington, *Outstanding
Women Members of Congress* (Washington, DC: United States Capitol Historical Society, 1995):
35.

p. 39: "I urge you . . . events of the day": "Commencement Address at Mount Holyoke College"
(speech, South Hadley, MA, June 1, 1975), Iowa State University Archives of Women's Political
Communication, https://awpc.cattcenter.iastate.edu/2018/10/10/commencement-address-at
-mount-holyoke-college-june-1-1975/.

Nikki Haley

p. 40: "Push through the fear": quoted in Ashley Parker, "How Much Sway Does Ambassador Nikki Haley Really Have Over President Trump?" *Glamour,* September 20, 2017, https://www.glamour.com/story/how-much-sway-does-ambassador-nikki-haley-really-have-over-president-trump.

p. 40: "When the daughter . . . still exists": Nikki Haley, *Can't Is Not an Option: My American Story* (New York: Sentinel, 2012), 237.

p. 41: "I love this . . . us strong": quoted in Ashley Parker, "How Much Sway."

p. 41: "I hope that . . . and security": ibid.

Fannie Lou Hamer

p. 42: "I am sick . . . tired": Fannie Lou Hamer, *The Speeches of Fannie Lou Hamer: To Tell It Like It Is,* ed. Maegan Parker Brooks and Davis W. Houck (Jackson: University Press of Mississippi, 2011), 62.

p. 43: "So whether you're . . . on our way": ibid., 83.

Kamala Harris

p. 44: "The American dream belongs to all of us": Kamala Harris, "Remarks at 2012 Democratic National Convention" (speech, Charlotte, NC, September 5, 2012), DNC 2012, September 6, 2012, video, 5:47, https://www.youtube.com/watch?v=zSmleiYaF-k.

p. 44: "My mother . . . not the last": Kamala Harris, "CNN Town Hall with Senator Kamala Harris," interview by Jake Tapper, CNN, January 28, 2019, https://www.cnn.com/politics/live-news/kamala-harris-town-hall-iowa/index.html.

p. 45: "Women have an . . . in our politics": quoted in Kayla Webley Adler, "We Have More Female Senators Than Ever Before — Here Are the Four New Ones to Watch," *Marie Claire,* February 13, 2017, https://www.marieclaire.com/culture/news/a25342/new-female-us-senators/.

Patricia Roberts Harris

p. 46: "If my life . . . the system": United States Senate, Committee on Banking, Housing and Urban Affairs, *Nomination of Patricia Roberts Harris to Be Secretary of the Department of Housing and Urban Development: Hearing Before the Committee on Banking, Housing and Urban Affairs,* January 10, 1977, 95th Cong. (Washington, DC: United States Government Printing Office, 1977), 41.

p. 47: "I feel deeply . . . considered before": quoted in "A Higher Standard: Patricia Roberts Harris," *Our American Story* (blog), National Museum of African American History and Culture, November 8, 2010, https://nmaahc.si.edu/blog-post/higher-standard-patricia-roberts-harris.

p. 47: "While there may be . . . forget it": United States Senate, *Nomination of Patricia Roberts Harris,* 41.

Carla Hayden

p. 48: "Remember this . . . be made": Carla Hayden, "Remarks by Carla Hayden, Librarian of Congress" (speech, Camden, NJ, May 17, 2017), Library of Congress, http://www.loc.gov/static

/portals/about/about-the-librarian/statements-and-multimedia/documents/2017may17
_hayden-rutgers.pdf.

p. 49: "As a descendant . . . historic moment": Carla Hayden, "Carla Hayden Sworn In as 14th
Librarian of Congress," Library of Congress, September 14, 2016, video, 32:30, https://www.loc
.gov/item/webcast-7403/.

Mazie Hirono
p. 50: "I've been . . . look like that": Mazie Hirono, "The Quiet Rage of Mazie Hirono," interview
by Nina Totenberg, *Morning Edition,* NPR, June 7, 2018, https://www.npr.org/2018/06/07
/617239314/the-quiet-rage-of-mazie-hirono.

p. 51: "If I had to . . . been picked": ibid.

p. 51: "I am a woman . . . that reaches people": quoted in Sydney Ember, "'I Believe Her': Mazie
Hirono Takes an Aggressive Stance in Kavanaugh Hearings," *New York Times,* September 25,
2018, https://www.nytimes.com/2018/09/25/us/politics/mazie-hirono-kavanaugh-senate.html.

Diane Humetewa
p. 52: "These types . . . hard work": quoted in Laurel Morales, "First Native American Woman to
Be a Federal Judge Takes Oath," KJZZ, May 19, 2014, https://kjzz.org/content/9635/first-native
-american-woman-be-federal-judge-takes-oath.

p. 53: "It is a proud . . . Native Americans": 160 Cong. Rec. S3018 (May 14, 2014) (statement of
Senator John McCain).

Kay Bailey Hutchison
p. 54: "I believe America . . . a woman": Kay Bailey Hutchison, introduction to *American Heroines:
The Spirited Women Who Shaped Our Country* (New York: William Morrow, 2004), xv.

p. 55: "Like most women . . . to work": quoted in Jan Jarboe Russell, "Sitting Pretty," *Texas
Monthly,* August 1994, https://www.texasmonthly.com/politics/sitting-pretty/.

p. 55: "I've had to fight . . . I get": ibid.

Barbara Jordan
p. 56: "The greatest motivation . . . inside you": quoted in Mary Beth Rogers, *Barbara Jordan:
American Hero* (New York: Bantam, 1998), 5.

p. 57: "We must provide . . . the future": Barbara Jordan, "1976 Democratic National Convention
Keynote Address" (speech, New York, NY, July 12, 1976), Iowa State University Archives of
Women's Political Communication, https://awpc.cattcenter.iastate.edu/2017/03/21/1976
-democratic-national-convention-keynote-address-july-12-1976/.

p. 57: "My presence here . . . be deferred": ibid.

Clare Boothe Luce
p. 58: "I don't think . . . what I like": quoted in Marie Brenner, "Fast and Luce," *Vanity Fair,* March
1988, https://www.vanityfair.com/news/1988/03/clare-boothe-luce-profile.

p. 59: "If I fail . . . what it takes'": quoted in Philip Nash, "A Woman's Place Is in the Embassy:

America's First Female Chiefs of Mission, 1933–1964," in *Women, Diplomacy and International Politics since 1500,* ed. Glenda Sluga and Carolyn James (New York: Routledge, 2016), 234.

Wilma Mankiller

p. 60: "No one told . . . they had tried": Wilma Mankiller and Michael Wallis, *Mankiller: A Chief and Her People* (New York: Macmillan, 2000), 112.

p. 60: "Prior to my becoming . . . become chief themselves": ibid., 246.

p. 61: "The most important . . . of the future": Wilma Mankiller, "Rebuilding the Cherokee Nation" (speech, Sweet Briar, VA, April 2, 1993), Iowa State University Archives of Women's Political Communication, https://awpc.cattcenter.iastate.edu/2017/03/21/rebuilding-the -cherokee-nation-april-2-1993/.

Susana Martinez

p. 62: "Growing up . . . todo es posible": Susana Martinez, "Remarks at the 2012 Republican National Convention" (speech, Tampa, FL, August 29, 2012), Iowa State University Archives of Women's Political Communication, https://awpc.cattcenter.iastate.edu/2017/03/09/remarks-at -the-2012-republican-national-convention-aug-29-2012/.

p. 63: "It's in moments . . . no more barriers": ibid.

p. 63: "Challenges shouldn't . . . to the task": Susana Martinez, "State of the State Address" (speech, Santa Fe, NM, January 18, 2011), Iowa State University Archives of Women's Political Communication, https://awpc.cattcenter.iastate.edu/2017/03/21/state-of-the-state-address -jan-18-2011/.

Patsy Takemoto Mink

p. 64: "I can't change . . . the future": quoted in "Hawaii's Patsy Mink Honored with Presidential Medal of Freedom," NBC, November 24, 2014, https://www.nbcnews.com/news/asian-america /hawaiis-patsy-mink-honored-presidential-medal-freedom-n248951.

p. 65: "No person . . . financial assistance": Title IX of the Education Amendments of 1972, 20 U.S.C. § 1681 (1972), https://www.justice.gov/crt/title-ix-education-amendments-1972.

p. 65: "I've run many . . . make the difference": *Patsy Mink: Ahead of the Majority,* directed by Kimberlee Bassford (San Francisco: ITVS, 2009), movie trailer, Women Make Movies, June 16, 2009, video, 1:52, https://www.youtube.com/watch?v=QsHncYl7Xcg.

p. 65: "Women's rights . . . justice": "Patsy Mink Speaks at 1984 Democratic National Convention" (speech, New York, NY, July 16, 1984), NBC Learn K-12 website, https://archives .nbclearn.com/portal/site/k-12/browse/?cuecard=4651.

Carol Moseley Braun

p. 66: "When women . . . color can win": Carol Moseley Braun, "Withdrawal from 2004 Presidential Race" (speech, Carroll, IA, January 15, 2004), Iowa State University Archives of Women's Political Communication, https://awpc.cattcenter.iastate.edu/2017/03/09/withdrawal -from-2004-presidential-race-jan-15-2004/.

p. 66: "the most important . . . to everybody": Carol Moseley Braun, "Leading Ladies: Sen. Carol

Moseley Braun," interview by Tony Cox, *News and Notes,* NPR, March 2, 2007, https://www.npr .org/templates/transcript/transcript.php?storyId=7678293.

p. 67: "My late mother . . . same boat now": "Full Transcript: Democratic Presidential Candidates Debate," *Washington Post,* September 9, 2003, http://www.washingtonpost.com/wp-srv/politics /transcripts/090903debatetext.html.

p. 67: "I ran for . . . be girls, too": Carol Moseley Braun, "Leading Ladies."

Alexandria Ocasio-Cortez
p. 68: "They'll tell you . . . do it anyway": Alexandria Ocasio-Cortez (@AOC), Twitter, March 9, 2018, 6:04 p.m., https://twitter.com/aoc/status/972292022362165249?lang=en.

p. 68: "Women like me . . . run for office": Alexandria Ocasio-Cortez (@AOC), Twitter, May 30, 2018, 5:01 a.m., video, 0:03, https://twitter.com/AOC/status/1001795660524457985.

p. 69: "In my opinion . . . our own house": quoted in Andrea González-Ramírez, "Meet the Bronx-Born Puerto Rican Challenging One of the Most Powerful House Democrats," Refinery29, June 27, 2018, https://www.refinery29.com/en-us/2018/06/201503/alexandria-ocasio-cortez-new -york-congress-14th-district.

p. 69: "I am running . . . pursue your dreams": Alexandria Ocasio-Cortez (ocasio2018), Instagram comment, June 23, 2017, https://www.instagram.com/p/BVr6nYzFX0u/.

Sandra Day O'Connor
p. 70: "The power I . . . my gender": quoted in Staci D. Kramer, "Enter O'Connor, Exit 'Mr. Justice,'" *New York Times,* November 16, 1990, https://www.nytimes.com/1990/11/16/news /enter-o-connor-exit-mr-justice.html.

p. 71: "Liberty requires . . . vantage points": Sandra Day O'Connor, *The Majesty of the Law: Reflections of a Supreme Court Justice* (New York: Random House, 2003), 276.

p. 71: "Freedom and equality . . . constant effort": ibid.

Nancy Pelosi
p. 72: "Get involved . . . and girls": Nancy Pelosi, *Know Your Power: A Message to America's Daughters* (New York: Doubleday, 2008), 128.

p. 73: "Organize, don't agonize": ibid., 70.

p. 73: "Know your . . . power, too": ibid., 174.

p. 73: "We have . . . make progress": Nancy Pelosi, "Remarks Upon Becoming Speaker of the House" (speech, Washington, DC, January 4, 2007), Iowa State University Archives of Women's Political Communication, https://awpc.cattcenter.iastate.edu/2017/03/21/remarks-upon -becoming-speaker-of-the-house-jan-4-2007/.

Frances Perkins
p. 74: "Feminism . . . a revolutionist": quoted in "Talk on Feminism Stirs Great Crowd," *New York Times,* February 18, 1914, 2, https://timesmachine.nytimes.com/timesmachine/1914/02/18 /100300396.html?pageNumber=2.

p. 75: "I had a kind . . . high seats": quoted in Emily Yellin, *Our Mothers' War: American Women at Home and at the Front During World War II* (New York: Free Press, 2004), 285.

Jeannette Rankin

p. 76: "Men and women . . . use both": quoted in Karen L. Owen, *Women Officeholders and the Role Models Who Pioneered the Way* (Lanham, MD: Lexington Books, 2017), 43.

p. 76: "I may be the . . . the last": quoted in "Jeannette Rankin," in *Women in Congress, 1917–2006* (Washington, DC: United States Government Printing Office, 2006), 37.

p. 77: "We're half the . . . the Congress": quoted in Hannah Josephson, *Jeannette Rankin: First Lady in Congress* (Indianapolis: Bobbs-Merrill, 1974), 197.

p. 77: "You can no more . . . an earthquake": ibid., 135.

Condoleezza Rice

p. 78: "In America . . . you are going": Condoleezza Rice, "Remarks at the 2000 Republican National Convention" (speech, Philadelphia, PA, August 1, 2000), Iowa State University Archives of Women's Political Communication, https://awpc.cattcenter.iastate.edu/2017/03/09/remarks-at-the-2000-rnc-aug-1-2000/.

p. 78: "Don't let anyone . . . those yourself": Condoleezza Rice, "Condoleezza Rice Tells Katie Couric, 'I Don't Miss Washington Very Much,'" interview by Katie Couric, *Glamour,* October 5, 2010, https://www.glamour.com/story/condoleezza-rice-tells-katie-couric-i-dont-miss-washington-very-much.

p. 79: "We need to . . . should be leaders": Condoleezza Rice (@CondoleezzaRice), Twitter, March 11, 2014, 11:45 a.m., https://twitter.com/condoleezzarice/status/443457701234745344?lang=en.

Eleanor Roosevelt

p. 80: "You must do . . . cannot do": Eleanor Roosevelt, *You Learn by Living* (New York: Harper Perennial, 2011), 30.

p. 81: "We must know . . . unpopularity": Eleanor Roosevelt, *Tomorrow Is Now: It Is Today That We Must Create the World of the Future* (New York: Penguin, 1963), 119.

Ileana Ros-Lehtinen

p. 82: "My advice . . . one word: start": Ileana Ros-Lehtinen, "In Her Footsteps: A Profile on Congresswoman Ileana Ros-Lehtinen," interview, United States Hispanic Chamber of Commerce website, April 17, 2018, https://ushcc.com/in-her-footsteps-a-profile-on-congresswoman-ileana-ros-lehtinen/.

p. 82: "I never thought . . . in Congress": Ileana Ros-Lehtinen, "Ileana Ros-Lehtinen, First Latina Elected to Congress," *Makers,* PBS, video, 0:42, https://www.makers.com/profiles/591f28904d21a8046c3a6382/554fb358e4b07729e36fb2cc.

p. 83: "My 'aha' moment . . . impact more individuals": Ileana Ros-Lehtinen, "In Her Footsteps."

p. 83: "for our brothers . . . democracy is like": quoted in Luis Feldstein Soto, "The Day Ileana Ros-

Lehtinen was Elected to Congress," *Miami Herald,* April 30, 2017, https://www.miamiherald.com /news/politics-government/article147721324.html.

p. 83: "No matter where . . . her dreams": Ileana Ros-Lehtinen, "Rep. Ros-Lehtinen on Advocating for Human Rights and Freedom Around the World," Heritage Foundation, July 18, 2011, video, 0:55, https://www.youtube.com/watch?v=Hm8pGb332Go.

p. 83: "ferocious she-wolf": Ashlee Anderson, "Ileana Ros-Lehtinen," National Women's History Museum, July 31, 2018, https://www.womenshistory.org/education-resources/biographies /ileana-ros-lehtinen.

Nellie Tayloe Ross
p. 84: "I shall expect . . . every case": "Nellie Tayloe Ross and None Other Will Be Governor of Wyoming," *Wyoming State Tribune and Cheyenne Daily Leader,* November 3, 1924, quoted in "This Day in Wyoming History: Nellie Tayloe Ross Elected Governor in 1924," *Wyoming Postscript: Musings of the Wyoming State Archives* (blog), November 5, 2014, https://wyostatearchives .wordpress.com/tag/womens-suffrage/.

p. 84: "Really, I dropped accidentally into politics": quoted in "Gov. Ross Laughs Over '28," *New York Times,* November 26, 1926, 15, https://timesmachine.nytimes.com/timesmachine/1926/11 /26/98525137.html?pageNumber=15.

p. 85: "The fact of my . . . to the people": "Nellie Tayloe Ross and None Other."

Susanna Madora Salter
p. 86: "Gentlemen, what is . . . presiding officer": quoted in Monroe Billington, "Susanna Madora Salter First Woman Mayor," *Kansas History* 21, no. 3 (Autumn 1954), 173–183, Kansas Historical Society, https://www.kshs.org/p/kansas-historical-quarterly-susanna-madora-salter/13106.

p. 87: "You were duly . . . notice thereof": ibid.

p. 87: "She declares she . . . eyes on Susanna": *New Haven Register,* May 6, 1887, 2, quoted in Tony Pettinato, "Prank Leads to Election of Nation's First Woman Mayor," Genealogy Bank blog, April 4, 2017.

p. 87: "Why, you look . . . other woman": quoted in Federal Writers' Project of the Work Projects Administration for the State of Kansas, *Kansas: A Guide to the Sunflower State* (New York: Viking, 1939), 430.

Lottie Shackelford
p. 88: "I truly enjoy . . . is all about": quoted in Vince Rodriguez, "Little Rock Mayor Is Black and Female," UPI, April 12, 1987, https://upi.com/4867581.

p. 88: "A lot of people . . . feeling of awe": ibid.

p. 89: "It's never about . . . yet to do": Lottie Shackelford, "Lottie H. Shackelford, Arkansas Women's Hall of Fame 2016 Honoree," Arkansas Women's Hall of Fame, October 24, 2016, video, 2:25, https://www.youtube.com/watch?v=ozsJ3we6WmY&feature=youtu.be.

p. 89: "We just gotta . . . county hall table": quoted in Terry Shropshire, "Lottie Shackelford Honored for Historic and Legendary Service in Arkansas Politics," *Rolling Out,* March 18, 2014, https://rollingout.com/2014/03/18/lottie-shackelford-honored-historic-service-arkansas-politics/.

Margaret Chase Smith

p. 90: "My answer is . . . everywhere": Margaret Chase Smith, foreword to *Outstanding Women Members of Congress,* by Shirley Washington (Washington, DC: United States Capitol Historical Society, 1995), 5.

p. 91: "The right way . . . moral character": Margaret Chase Smith, "We Must Not Forfeit Freedom," *Journal of the National Education Association* 41, no. 5 (1952), 300.

p. 91: "When people keep . . . to try it": "Nation: Madam Candidate," *Time,* February 7, 1964, 23.

Sonia Sotomayor

p. 92: "I do know one . . . define my worth": quoted in Nina Totenberg, "A Justice Deliberates: Sotomayor on Love, Health and Family," *Morning Edition,* NPR, January 12, 2013, https://www.npr.org/2013/01/14/167699633/a-justice-deliberates-sotomayor-on-love-health-and-family.

pp. 92–93: "The challenges . . . uncommon achievements": Sonia Sotomayor, preface to *My Beloved World* (New York: Knopf, 2013), viii.

p. 93: "Understand that failure . . . because of it": Sonia Sotomayor, "Sonia Speaks: An Interview with Justice Sonia Sotomayor," *The Progressive,* interview by Kevin Uhrich, February 9, 2013, https://progressive.org/dispatches/sonia-speaks-interview-justice-sonia-sotomayor/.

p. 93: "You can't dream . . . the possibilities are": quoted in Victoria A. F. Camron, "Boulder County Students Admire Justice Sotomayor's Accomplishments," *Longmont (CO) Times-Call,* May 2, 2013, http://www.timescall.com/ci_23157839/boulder-county-students-admire-justice-sotomayors-accomplishments.

Elizabeth Cady Stanton

p. 94: "No country ever . . . in the government": Elizabeth Cady Stanton, *Selected Papers of Elizabeth Cady Stanton and Susan B. Anthony,* ed. Ann D. Gordon, vol. 1, (New Jersey: Rutgers University Press, 1997), 551.

p. 95: "The right is . . . secure this right": ibid., 105.

p. 95: "We hold these . . . created equal": *First Convention Ever Called to Discuss the Civil and Political Rights of Women, Seneca Falls, New York, July 19, 20, 1848,* Library of Congress, https://www.loc.gov/item/rbcmiller001107/.

Mary Church Terrell

p. 96: "And so, lifting . . . upward we go": Mary Church Terrell, *The Progress of Colored Women* (speech, Washington, DC, February 18, 1898) (Washington, DC: Smith Brothers, 1898), 15, Daniel Murray Pamphlet Collection and African American Pamphlet Collection, Library of Congress, https://www.loc.gov/item/90898298/.

p. 97: "All during my . . . of my race": Mary Church Terrell, *A Colored Woman in a White World* (Washington, DC: Ransdell, 1940), 60.

p. 97: "We knock at . . . an equal chance": Mary Church Terrell, *The Progress,* 15.

p. 97: "I will take . . . privileges and rights": Mary Church Terrell, *A Colored Woman,* 426.

Elizabeth Warren

p. 98: "Keep just a little . . . regret it": Elizabeth Warren, "Springfield College Commencement Address" (speech, Springfield, MA, May 19, 2013), Springfield College, May 30, 2013, video, 12:15, https://www.youtube.com/watch?v=q7enEzLi0y4.

p. 99: "Women vote . . . and win": quoted in Kelcey Caulder, "Warren Hits Back at Trump: 'He's Trying to Bully All Women and Make Us All Shut Up,'" *Independent Journal Review,* July 7, 2018, https://ijr.com/warren-trump-fighting/.

p. 99: "She was warned . . . persisted": quoted in Matt Flegenheimer, "Republican Senators Vote to Formally Silence Elizabeth Warren," *New York Times,* February 7, 2017, https://www.nytimes.com/2017/02/07/us/politics/republican-senators-vote-to-formally-silence-elizabeth-warren.html?module=inline.

Ida B. Wells-Barnett

p. 100: "The people must . . . with the press": Ida B. Wells, *Southern Horrors and Other Writings,* ed. Jacqueline Jones Royster (New York: Bedford, 1996), 70.

p. 101: "The way to right . . . truth upon them": Ida B. Wells, *The Light of Truth: Writings of an Anti-Lynching Crusader,* ed. Mia Bay (New York: Penguin, 2014), xix.

Edith Wilson

p. 102: "All the threads . . . minutes": Edith Bolling Wilson to Woodrow Wilson, August 13, 1915, Edith Bolling Wilson Letters, Woodrow Wilson Presidential Library and Museum, http://presidentwilson.org/items/show/8687.

p. 103: "A completely gifted woman": Woodrow Wilson, *The Papers of Woodrow Wilson,* vol. 33 (Princeton, NJ: Princeton University Press, 1980), 118.

Victoria Woodhull

p. 104: "Women have every . . . exercise them": Victoria Claflin Woodhull and Tennessee C. Claflin, *The Human Body the Temple of God* (London, 1890), 298.

p. 105: "What is there . . . future government": Victoria C. Woodhull, "The New Rebellion: The Great Secession Speech" (speech, New York, NY, May 11, 1871), in Paulina W. Davis, *A History of the National Woman's Rights Movement, for Twenty Years* (New York, 1871), 117, Susan B. Anthony Collection and National American Woman Suffrage Association Collection, Library of Congress, https://www.loc.gov/item/03026134/.

How to Stand Up, Speak Out, and Make a Difference: A Take-Action Guide

p. 107: "Real change . . . step at a time": United States Senate, Committee on the Judiciary, *Nomination of Ruth Bader Ginsburg to Be Associate Justice of the Supreme Court of the United States: Hearings Before the Committee on the Judiciary,* July 20, 21, 22, and 23, 1993, 103rd Cong. (Washington, DC: United States Government Printing Office, 1994), 122.

ACKNOWLEDGMENTS

We have so many talented, inspirational people to thank for the creation of this dream of a book. Karen Lotz is truly an editor extraordinaire. Your enthusiasm, insights, support, and dedication have lifted us up, carried us through, and made the whole process a joy. Thank you, Kylie Akia and Alexandra Bye, for gracing the book with your inspiring art. Phoebe Kosman, you are creative, diligent, and awesome. Let's hear it for suffragette yellow! Lydia Abel, thank you for your hard work on this book as well.

Honestly, the entire team at Candlewick is exceptional. Thank you, Hannah Mahoney, for being an amazing copy chief and supporter of this book. We are so appreciative of the entire editorial services crew: Kate Hurley, Martha Dwyer, Jackie Houton, Emily Quill, Maggie Deslaurier, JoAnne Sweeney, Sally Bratcher, and Erin Jones. Thank you to Matt Roeser for a fantastic jacket design, to Lisa Rudden for the fabulous interior design and art direction, and to Sherry Fatla for her creative and art direction. A shout-out to the people in production for keeping a close and watchful eye on everything and making miracles happen when needed: Gregg Hammerquist, Amanda Bellamy, Sarah Sherman, and Kim Lanza. And big thanks for editorial assistance from Olivia Swomley and Alice McConnell. Cheers to Frankie Knuckles and Analía Cabello for your work on the book as well. Making a book is a team effort, and we love being part of Team Candlewick. Thank you for making it possible to share the stories of these women with the world.

Sincere thanks and reverence to Hillary Rodham Clinton for contributing the foreword to the book and for inspiring so many girls to dream big. And many thanks to Huma Abedin, Nick Merrill, and Robert Russo for your time and careful eye. Dorothy McAuliffe, your support and encouragement have been invaluable and are so very much appreciated.

Thank you, Adriana Domínguez of Full Circle Literary, for wholeheartedly backing *Leading the Way* every step of the way. We are lucky to have you in our lives. ¡Agentísima!

Thank you to Jefferson County Library for allowing us to get our hands on so many wonderful sources. Libraries rock!

Kappy Kling, thank you for providing all the wonders a local bookstore can bestow upon a community: a place to meet, a place to share news, books, coffee, and support for local authors.

Janet sends a special thanks to her husband, Hunt Howell, for always supporting her and her dreams in every way, and to her parents, Ed and Elsie Denison, who convinced her she could do anything a boy could do, even when her schools taught the opposite. And she says thank you as well to Karol Straub, for keeping her on task during long legislative days.

From Theresa: Special thanks to Jennifer McGrath, Margret Principe, Marlo Naumer, and Kelli Perry for their friendship and for being my village while I worked on this project. Thank you, Lora Morini, Mary Dewinkeleer, and Monica Matulonis, for being fierce friends throughout the years and forever. Mom, thank you for being a lifelong inspiration, for loving me for who I am, for your quiet and unwavering support, and for giving me my love of books. I love you and Emily, the two most special women in my life. Thank you, Brian, for believing in me. Ella and Sylvia, thank you for brightening my life. Watching you grow and bravely take life on is my greatest joy.

Last, gigantic, enormous, sincerest thanks to all the women in the book. Yours are the shoulders we stand on. We see you. Thank you for leading the way.

ABOUT THE CREATORS

SENATOR JANET HOWELL has been a Virginia state senator since 1992. She is second in seniority in the state senate and the longest-serving female Virginia legislator. Credited with major legal reforms, she was also the first woman to serve on the powerful Senate Finance Committee and the first and only woman so far to be appointed as a senate budget conferee. A civil rights worker in college and a longtime community leader, she has been honored with many awards, including a Child Health Advocate Award from the American Academy of Pediatrics. She lives in northern Virginia with her husband, Hunt.

photo by Bill Moree

KYLIE AKIA is a digital illustrator and painter. *Leading the Way: Women in Power* is her picture book debut. She lives in Chicago.

THERESA HOWELL is the coauthor, with F. Isabel Campoy, of the award-winning book *Maybe Something Beautiful,* illustrated by Rafael López. She is also the author of the picture book series Scout Moore: Junior Ranger. She lives in Colorado with her two daughters and her husband, Brian.

photo by Meghan Hof

ALEXANDRA BYE creates illustrations in various media for a range of outlets, including magazines and children's publications. She lives in New Hampshire.

photo by Alex Tourigny

INDEX OF PEOPLE